WITHDRAWN

D1385702

Guide to Part L
of the Building Regulations

Conservation of fuel and power

2010 Edition

LRC Stoke Park
GUILDFORD COLLEGE

bre

181592
692. 9 BUI
OTBTA.

© RIBA Enterprises Ltd, 2010

Published by NBS, 15 Bonhill Street, London EC2P 2EA

ISBN 978 1 85946 363 5

Stock code 72387

The right of BRE to be identified as the Author of this Work has been asserted in accordance with the Copyright, Design and Patents Act 1988.

All rights reserved. No part of this publication may be reproduced, stored in a retrieval system, or transmitted, in any form or by any means, electronic, mechanical, photocopying, recording or otherwise, without prior permission of the copyright owner.

British Library Cataloguing in Publication Data
A catalogue record for this book is available from the British Library.

Publisher: Steven Cross
Commissioning Editor: Lucy Harbor
Project Editor: Prepress Projects Ltd, Perth, UK
Designed by Philip Handley
Typeset by Prepress Projects Ltd, Perth, UK
Printed and bound by Thanet Press, Margate, UK

While every effort has been made to check the accuracy and quality of the information given in this publication, neither the Author nor the Publisher accept any responsibility for the subsequent use of this information, for any errors or omissions that it may contain, or for any misunderstandings arising from it.

NBS is part of RIBA Enterprises Ltd.
www.thenbs.com
www.ribaenterprises.com

Contents

Foreword

Designing energy-efficient buildings is the foundation stone of good design and it is crucial for architects to understand and evaluate performance during the design process. It is now commonly accepted that increasing carbon dioxide (CO_2) emissions from burning fossil fuels has a direct relationship to climate change. Given the significance of CO_2 emissions from buildings as a proportion of our national total, it is encouraging that the government has identified the building sector as a key element in its overall carbon reduction strategy. The government's commitment to introduce increasingly stringent legislation in this area is signalled through its ambition for new housing to be zero carbon from 2016 and similarly for other buildings from 2019. To support this objective, the government will revise Part L of the Building Regulations every three years to raise standards for energy efficiency, promote the use of **low- and zero-carbon (LZC) energy supply systems** and introduce further measures to address carbon emissions from buildings.

The new Approved Documents (ADs) build on the flexible approach that was introduced with the 2006 revisions, in which demonstrating compliance is based on calculations of the building's CO_2 emissions, rather than on prescriptive solutions. The 2010 revisions will typically result in a 25% reduction in building carbon emissions relative to the previous standards, although the target reduction varies for different types of building.

For the first time, the public consultation for the revisions to the ADs was accompanied by a 'Future Thinking' paper to provide an initial view of the way Part L might evolve after 2010. For new homes, targets for CO_2 emissions will be reduced by a further 25% in 2013. As emissions targets are tightened and we reach the limits of performance that can be achieved through energy efficiency alone, renewable systems are likely to play an increasingly important role. The 'Future Thinking' paper introduced the concept of 'Allowable Solutions': to address carbon emissions that cannot be reduced on the site of the development.

Thankfully, this revised guide unpicks any unfamiliar new requirements. Aimed to serve the needs of the designer, *Guide to Part L of the Building Regulations* comprises a series of invaluable flowcharts for each of the four new documents, all of which are backed up with guidance that amplifies important points and clarifies meanings. This is supported by extensive appendices that explain some of the science, concepts and processes that are required in order to comply. Usefully, there is also a comprehensive bibliography, not only of the **second-tier documents** and **third-tier documents** referred to in Part L but also of many others that are central to good practice. I can see it becoming a genuinely important reference work for architects, construction professionals and building control officers as they grapple with the new approach. I thoroughly recommend it to you.

Alan Shingler
of Sheppard Robson
Chair of the RIBA Sustainable Futures Committee and the RIBA President's
Advisor on Sustainability
September 2010

General introduction

0.1 Introduction to the guide

The busy designer, whether a sole practitioner or a team member in a large global organisation, may not have time to study and understand in detail all the relevant legislation. This guide is intended to be at the designer's side to provide an immediate source of advice when time is precious and deadlines have to be met.

The layout provides quick access to the essentials so that they can be assimilated easily, without cluttering the text with superfluous detail. The following two types of highlighting are used:

 ESSENTIAL

> To aid rapid digestion of the key points, boxes like this contain fundamental material and mandatory requirements.

Readers requiring more details and explanation of a particular area of interest can find these in the appendices.

 FOR INFORMATION

> Useful background information and points of interest are in boxes like this.

Words highlighted in **bold** have a specific technical meaning that is explained in the Glossary section of this guide.

The requirements of the Part L ADs are difficult to assimilate and apply. The authors have spent many man-hours – on the reader's behalf – looking into the meaning and importance of each clause in the ADs, researching the cross-references and compiling the guidance. Where cross-reference documents are not available, the guide aims to either fill in the gaps or provide alternative solutions.

There is repetition in the four sections that constitute the Part L ADs, so this guide is designed to give a quick 'road map' overview of each section. Detailed guidance on any particular subject can mostly be found in the appendices.

The guide cannot cover every conceivable design approach, so, where we have included 'deemed to satisfy' solutions, they are fairly traditional. Highly specialised or individual approaches to meeting the requirements of the regulations are permitted, subject to satisfying the criteria, but we have not attempted to cover them here.

Every effort has been made to ensure the accuracy of the information included in this guide at the time of publication; however, legislation is constantly being revised and updated and there are likely to be amendments to the ADs themselves. Readers will have ultimate responsibility for ensuring that they have taken account of all the most up-to-date requirements of the appropriate legislation.

0.2   Background

The revision of the Part L ADs is an outcome of the government's *Building a Greener Future: Policy Statement* (July 2007).[1] This confirms the government's intention for all new homes to be zero carbon by 2016 along with a major progressive tightening of the energy efficiency Building Regulations – by 25% in 2010 and by 44% in 2013. The 2008 budget announced an ambition for new buildings other than **dwellings** to be zero carbon from 2019, with a similar 25% reduction in 2010. The government is also committed to addressing the energy efficiency of existing buildings.

The proposed energy efficiency standards are likely to result in more airtight buildings and so it is necessary to amend the Part F of the Building Regulations[2] at the same time to ensure that adequate ventilation is provided.

0.3   What the Building Regulations actually require

Building Regulations require that all buildings are energy efficient, have their building services fitted with effective controls and are properly commissioned. In addition, the householder or building owner needs to be given sufficient information on the building, the fixed building services and their maintenance requirements so that the building can be operated efficiently, using no more fuel and power 'than is reasonable in the circumstances'.

The Building Regulations apply to all building types. The ADs, which contain guidance on how the requirements would typically be complied with, are divided into four sections to differentiate between dwellings and other buildings and to further differentiate between new **building work** and work to existing buildings in each group.

The Building Regulations (2000) and subsequent amendments require that **'reasonable provision'** should be made for the conservation of fuel and power in buildings that use energy to condition the indoor climate[3] by:

- limiting heat gains and losses through **thermal elements** and other parts of the building fabric;
- limiting heat gains and losses from pipes, ducts and vessels used for space heating, space cooling and hot water storage;
- providing energy-efficient fixed building services, which have effective controls and which have been properly commissioned to deliver their specified functional performance and use no more fuel and power than is necessary;
- providing the owner with sufficient information about the building, building services and their maintenance so that it can be operated to minimise the use of fuel and power as much as is reasonable in the circumstances.

The ADs contain guidance and indicate reasonable provision for meeting these requirements.

For all new buildings, the calculated **dwelling emission rate (DER)** for dwellings and the **building emission rate (BER** – the amount of CO_2 emitted per year by non-domestic buildings and dwellings over 450m^2) for other types of building must be based on the actual building design and be no greater than the calculated **target emission rate (TER** – this outlines the minimum energy performance requirement for new dwellings in kilograms of CO_2 emitted per year).

If there is any change in the energy status of a building, the Regulations now require that reasonable provision should be made to improve the energy performance of thermal elements that are being renovated or renewed (Regulation 4A), even though they may be neither part of a **material alteration** nor regarded as building work as defined in Regulation 3. As such, they do not need to comply with the other technical requirements of the Regulations (Parts A–P inclusive).

Regulation 17D requires **consequential improvement works** to existing buildings in some circumstances.

Regulation 20B makes it mandatory that new buildings, including dwellings, are tested for air leakage to demonstrate that the construction meets the design assumptions. This greatly extends the requirements under the previous Regulation 18, which made testing an option.

Regulation 20C requires a formal certificate to show that the commissioning of heating and hot water systems has been carried out by a Part J or Part P **approved competent person** in the case of dwellings or by a **suitably qualified person** in the case of other types of buildings. It should be noted that a commissioning plan is produced at the design stage, and that this must be followed throughout construction.

Note that the requirements of other parts of the Regulations must still be satisfied when meeting the requirements of Part L. Part F, for instance, describes requirements for ventilation that should not conflict with the requirements for limiting air leakage under Part L. In certain circumstances, alterations to the structure of a building under Part A, fire protection under Part B or access to and use of buildings under Part M, which change the energy status of a building (see AD L1B 4.12, AD L2B 4.16), will mean that improvements to the energy performance of thermal elements and/or **controlled services** or **controlled fittings** will be required under Part L.

0.4   Changes since the previous edition

The 2010 revisions to the ADs emphasise the distinction between the requirements and guidance, recognising that the guidance may not be applicable if a building is unusual in some way. Therefore, there is no obligation to adopt any particular solution contained in the ADs if it would be preferred to meet the relevant requirement in some other way, but proposed solutions should always be checked by building control bodies (BCBs) for compliance with Building Regulations.

The main changes introduced in 2010 are summarised below and set out in detail at the beginning of each of the four sections of Part L:

General changes

*   emphasis of the distinction between the requirements set out in the Building Regulations and the guidance set out in the ADs;
*   removal of the exemptions from the energy efficiency requirements [Regulations 9(3) to 9(6)] but inclusion of specific guidance on what is reasonable provision with respect to the building work currently listed there (e.g. for buildings with low levels of heating, new buildings with a planned life of less than two years and existing **historic buildings**);
*   clarification that the requirements apply to all conditioned spaces and are not just for the purposes of providing human comfort; and
*   rise in standards of energy and carbon efficiency.

New buildings

*   definition of standards for swimming pool basins (dwellings and non-domestic buildings);
*   requirement of a design-stage calculation of carbon emissions as a means of improving compliance (dwellings and non-domestic buildings);
*   requirement that a commissioning plan be made available with the deposit of plans (dwellings and non-domestic buildings);
*   change in the basis of the notional building used to determine the TER (non-domestic buildings) – an aggregate approach has been introduced that is expected to achieve a 25% reduction in carbon emissions across all new non-domestic buildings, but the reduction achieved will vary between building types;
*   revision of guidance for shell and core developments (non-domestic buildings);
*   revision of procedures for limiting the effect of solar gain in the summer (non-domestic buildings); and

- introduction of guidance for the installation of renewable energy systems plans (dwellings and non-domestic buildings).

Existing buildings

- energy efficiency requirements now apply to any building space where energy is used to condition the indoor climate, and not just those that are occupied;
- some **conservatories** smaller than 30m² will now need to comply with Part L;
- definition of standards for swimming pool basins (dwellings and non-domestic buildings);
- revision of guidance on the first fit-out of shell and core developments;
- definition of standards for swimming pool basins;
- removal of exemptions for conservatories with areas less than 30m²; and
- revised definition of **renovation**.

0.5   Which section of Part L?

The following is a brief summary to help readers to find the appropriate section of the guide quickly. It may also help to refer to Table 1 of this guide. Specific guidance applies to historic buildings or buildings in conservation areas, national parks or areas of outstanding natural beauty.

If you are modifying, but not extending, an existing building, then any new or replacement windows, roof lights, roof windows or doors and any new space heating, hot water service boilers, air conditioning or mechanical ventilation in the building is within the remit of these regulations. It also includes the requirement in certain circumstances to improve the energy performance when replacing or renovating walls, floors or roofs.

AD L1A *Conservation of Fuel and Power in New Dwellings* (2010 edition) applies to new-build dwellings such as houses and flats (or if attached to a dwelling a space for commercial use that could at some stage revert to being a dwelling; see AD L1A 3.3.

AD L1B *Conservation of Fuel and Power in Existing Dwellings* covers **extensions to a dwelling** (including conservatories) and material alterations to existing dwellings, as well as dwellings created by a **material change of use**. It also applies to work on certain services or fittings (called controlled services or fittings) such as new external doors or windows, new hot water systems, mechanical ventilation and cooling systems, insulation of existing pipes and ducts, lighting or the provision of a new or changed thermal element (wall, roof or floor). Under certain circumstances, work in existing dwellings can trigger consequential improvement works.

AD L2A *Conservation of Fuel and Power in New Buildings other than Dwellings* covers new buildings other than dwellings, including the first **fit-out works** to a building. This part covers heated common areas in residential buildings as well as nursing homes, student accommodation and, in mixed-use developments, the commercial or retail space. It also includes extensions of areas greater than 100m² and greater than 25% of the existing floor area.

AD L2B *Conservation of Fuel and Power in Existing Buildings other than Dwellings* covers **consequential improvement works** (required when adding an extension or changing a service to a building with a useful area of more than 1000m²), extensions to a dwelling, material alterations, material changes of use or changes in the energy status of existing buildings as well as replacements of certain services or fittings (called controlled services or controlled fittings) such as new external doors or windows, new hot water systems, mechanical ventilation and cooling systems, lighting and insulation of existing pipes and ducts, or provision of a new or changed thermal element (wall, roof or floor).

Take care, because AD L2A also covers heated common areas in residential buildings as well as nursing homes, student accommodation and – in mixed-use developments – the commercial or retail space. It also includes extensions that are both over 100m² AND greater than 25% of the existing floor area.

Table 1 lists the appropriate Part L for the range of options that are described within the AD.

If you follow the guidance in the Part L ADs, this would fulfil the requirements of the Building Regulations in the following clauses:

- 4A (renovated or replaced thermal elements to comply with requirements);
- 4B (where there is a change of energy status);
- 9 (guidance for building types that were previously exempt from the requirements)
- 17A (the requirement for a methodology to calculate the energy performance of a building);
- 17B (the requirement to set minimum energy performance requirements in the form of target CO_2 emissions);
- 17C (any new building shall meet the target CO_2 emission rate);
- 17D (extensions or provision of, or increased capacity to, new fixed building services in buildings over 1000m² are to comply with the requirements of Part L if technically and economically feasible);

- 17E/F [provision and registration of Energy Performance Certificates (EPCs)];
- 20B (ensure, give notice and confirm that pressure testing has been carried out and recorded);
- 20C (provide notice by a certain date that all fixed building services have been properly commissioned); and
- 20D (provide a notice to the local authority that specifies the target CO_2 emission rate for the building and the calculated CO_2 rate for the building as constructed).

Table 1
Which part of Part L?

New build	Existing	Use of space	Use Part
Dwelling		House or flat	L1A
	Extension to a dwelling	House or flat	L1B
Commercial space (or office) in a dwelling that could revert to domestic use		If there is direct access from the dwelling to the commercial space, both are within the same thermal envelope and the living space is a substantial proportion of the whole area of the building	L1A
New building other than dwellings		Not a house or flat. Refer below in this table for buildings that are exempt	L2A
	New non-dwelling extension of more than 100m² AND more than 25% of existing gross floor area	Not a house, a flat or a room used as a dwelling. Refer below in this table for buildings that are exempt	L2A
	New non-dwelling extension of less than 100m²	Not a house, a flat or a room used as a dwelling. Refer below in this table for buildings that are exempt	L2B

Table 1
Continued

New build	Existing	Use of space	Use Part
	New non-dwelling extension less than 25% of existing gross floor area	Not a house, a flat or a room used as a dwelling. Refer below in this table for buildings that are exempt	L2B
	Dwelling created as part of a material change of use	House or flat	L1B
	Provision of controlled fittings	House or flat	L1B
	Provision of controlled services	House or flat	L1B
	Material alteration to existing dwelling	House or flat	L1B
	Renovation of thermal element	House or flat	L1B
	Unheated common parts	Flats only	L1B
Unheated common parts		Where common parts serve a mixed development including flats	L2A
	Unheated common parts	Where common parts serve a mixed development including flats	L2B
Heated common parts		Flats only	L2A
Heated common parts		Where common parts serve a mixed development including flats	L2A
	Heated common parts	Where common parts serve a mixed development including flats; all building types including flats	L2B

Table 1
Continued

New build	Existing	Use of space	Use Part
Nursing home		Accommodation	L2A
	Nursing home	Accommodation	L2B
Student accommodation		Accommodation	L2A
	Student accommodation	Accommodation	L2B
Hostel		Accommodation	L2A
	Hostel	Accommodation	L2B
Hotel		Accommodation	L2A
	Hotel	Accommodation	L2B
	Conservatory/glazed extension smaller than 30m²	Attached to thermal envelope of house or flat	L1B or exempt*
	Conservatory/glazed extension greater than 30m²	Attached to thermal envelope of house or flat	L1B
	Conservatory/glazed extension smaller than 30m²	Attached to, but outside, thermal envelope of any building other than dwelling	L2B or exempt*
	Conservatory/glazed extension greater than 30m²	Attached to, but outside, thermal envelope of any building other than dwelling	L2B
	Enclosing an existing courtyard or under an extended roof	Not a dwelling	L2B

Table 1
Continued

New build	Existing	Use of space	Use Part
	Historic monument or building	House or flat	L1B
	Historic monument or building	Other than house or flat	L2B
Places of worship such as churches, mosques, synagogues and temples	Places of worship such as churches, mosques, synagogues and temples	This does not include 'buildings used for religious activity' that have additional functions	Exempt
Temporary building with a planned life of less than two years			Exempt, but follow *Energy Performance Standards for Modular Buildings*
Modular building constructed of more than 70% prefabricated sub-assemblies from centrally held or disassembled stock manufactured before April 2006			Exempt, but follow *Energy Performance Standards for Modular Buildings*
Modular buildings		Other than those described in the preceding two rows	L2A
Industrial sites with a low energy demand	Industrial sites with a low energy demand	The regulations do not cover the energy consumed directly by a commercial or industrial process	Exempt
Non-residential agricultural buildings with a low energy demand	Non-residential agricultural buildings with a low energy demand		Exempt

Table 1
Continued

New build	Existing	Use of space	Use Part
Residential buildings used less than four months of the year			L1A
	Residential buildings used less than four months of the year		L1B
Stand-alone buildings with an area of less than 50m²	Stand-alone buildings with an area of less than 50m²	Not a dwelling	Exempt
Stand-alone dwelling with an area of less than 50m²			L1A
	Stand-alone dwelling with an area of less than 50m²		L2B
Initial fit-out works	Existing building or shell and core development	A new EPC is required for the part of the building covered by the fit-out	L2A

*Where the building fabric that separates the conservatory from the building is retained or, if removed, is replaced to new standards for energy efficiency, and where the heating system of the building is not extended into the conservatory.

0.6 Further help

If you do not understand the technical guidance or other information set out in this guide or the ADs, there are a number of routes through which you can seek further assistance:

- the Communities and Local Government (CLG) website: www. communities.gov.uk;[4]
- the Planning Portal website: www.planningportal.gov.uk;
- your local authority building control service or your approved inspector (depending on which building control service you are using, or intend to use, to certify compliance of your work with the requirements of the Building Regulations);
- businesses registered with an approved competent person self-certification scheme/scheme operators; and
- specialists or industry bodies with expertise in the area of concern.

Notes

1. *Building a Greener Future: Policy Statement.* CLG (July 2007).
2. *Building Regulations Part F – Means of Ventilation.* CLG (2010).
3. BRE Report BR 262 *Thermal Insulation: Avoiding Risks.* BRE (2001).
4. See http://www.communities.gov.uk/planningandbuilding/buildingregulations/competentpersons-schemes/

AD L1A: new dwellings

AD L1A *Conservation of Fuel and Power in New Dwellings* (2010 edition) applies to new-build **dwellings** such as houses and flats (or if attached to a dwelling a space for commercial use that could at some stage revert to being a dwelling; see AD L1A 3.3.

1.1   Summary of 2010 changes to AD L1A

The main revisions to AD L1A made in 2010 are summarised below:

1.   clearer distinctions made between the requirements of the regulations and the guidance contained within the ADs;
2.   standards defined for swimming pool basins in new dwellings (see 1.3.2 of this guide);
3.   design-stage **TER/BER** calculation required as a means of helping to improve compliance (see 5.1.2 of this guide);
4.   revised guidance on demonstrating **reasonable provision** for the continuity of insulation (see 1.3.3 of this guide);
5.   commissioning plan required to be made available with deposit of plans (see 1.3.14); and
6.   higher standards of performance generally.

1.2   The five criteria

All five criteria have to be met. Energy-efficient measures should not compromise the other requirements of the Building Regulations.

The criteria are:

1.   achieving the TER: predicted rate of CO_2 emissions (**DER**) should be less than the TER;
2.   limits on design flexibility: thermal performance of building fabric and performance of fixed building services should be no worse than the design limits set out in AD L1A;
3.   limiting the effects of solar gains in summer: passive solar control measures should be provided;

4. building performance consistent with DER: as-built performance should be consistent with the predictions; and

5. provisions for energy-efficient operation of the dwelling: easily understood guidance to occupiers on energy-efficient operation of their systems should be provided.

1.3 A simple road map for compliance

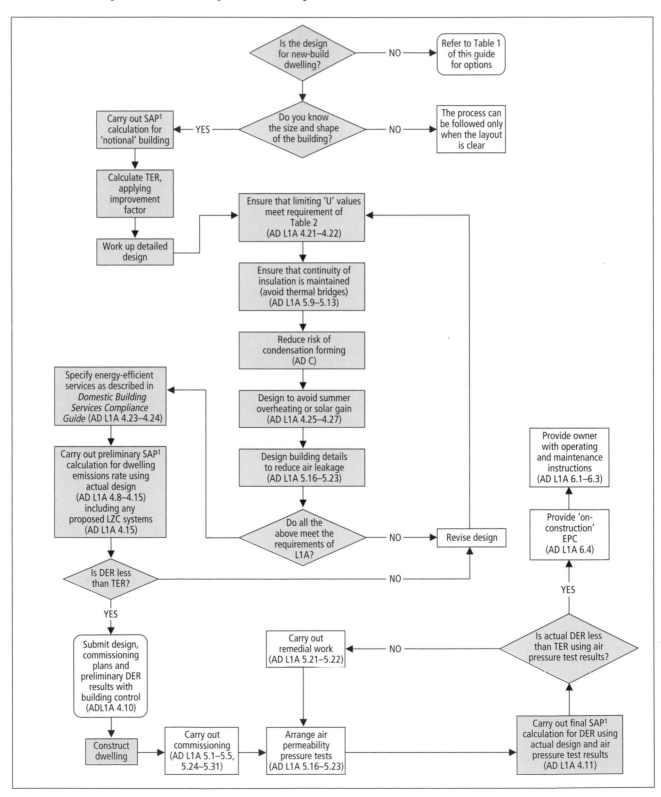

Figure 1
Road map for compliance

By following this map, you will be able to determine how to meet the requirements of the Building Regulations for new dwellings. The broad principles are:

(a) reduce energy demand:
   i. meet remaining energy demands with high-efficiency systems;
   ii. use low-carbon energy supplies and systems; and
(b) provide operating instructions and monitoring facilities so that occupants can manage their energy use.

The map includes items that are to be produced by 'the builder'; however, in practice the designer would have to design and specify solutions that allow the builder to meet the requirements.

The process outlined below follows the order that the designer is likely to follow rather than the order of the criteria in L1A.

1.3.1   Work out your target emissions (target emission rate)

Regulation 17C requires that where a new building is erected its predicted CO_2 emissions must not exceed the TER.

Criterion 1: Achieving the TER

The TER is expressed as the mass of CO_2 in kilograms emitted per square metre of floor area per year as the result of the provision of heating, cooling, hot water, ventilation and internal fixed lighting from a notional dwelling (i.e. of the same size and shape as the intended dwelling but using specified values for the energy performance of fabric and services, adjusted for the type of fuel used). The TER represents the minimum energy performance required to meet the regulations.

The predicted DER, based on the building as constructed, must be no worse than the TER when calculated using the same methodology (details of the information required and how this is actually done are included in Appendix 5.1). The TER for a dwelling designed to AD L1A 2010 will be 25% less than one meeting the 2006 standards.

The Government's Standard Assessment Procedure for the Energy Rating of Dwellings (SAP) must be used for the calculation of the TER and the DER, and these calculations must be certified by an **accredited SAP assessor**. The text, tables and worksheet can be downloaded from http://www.bre.co.uk/sap2009.[1] The same web page also carries the list of approved software implementations of SAP 2009.

Note that, on completion of the building, the builder will be required to notify building control that an EPC has been logged on the national register. This must be done by an accredited domestic energy assessor; it may be appropriate to employ this expert for all the calculations required under Part L.

Please refer to Appendix 5.1 for details.

1.3.2   Ensure that U-values comply

Criterion 2: Limits on design flexibility

Table 2 in AD L1A sets out the worst acceptable U-values for the area-weighted average of each element type. It is important to check that all U-values in the design meet these minimum levels. These levels are unchanged from the values set in 2006, so it is now even more likely that these U-values will have to be bettered in order to meet the TER.

U-values shall be calculated using the methods and conventions as set out in BR 443.[2] It is also important to check details and calculations to rule out the risk of interstitial condensation (BR 262).[3]

Please refer to Appendix 5.6 for details.

Where a swimming pool is constructed as part of a new dwelling, heat loss from the pool basin should be no worse than 0.25W/m²·K, and, for the purposes of calculating TER and DER, the dwelling should be assessed by assuming that the area covered by the pool is replaced with the equivalent area of floor with the same U-value as the pool surround.

AD L1A introduced new guidance for party walls and other thermal bypasses to restrict air movement through the air cavity – either by fully filling the cavity and/or by providing effective sealing around the perimeter.

1.3.3   Ensure that thermal bridges comply

Criterion 2: Limits on design flexibility

At the internal surfaces, where insulation is discontinuous or is insufficient (window frames and reveals at the eaves and so on), the effectiveness of the provided insulation is reduced and cool spots are created, allowing heat to escape and increasing the risk of condensation on the inner surface. This brings with it a host of problems including wood rot, crumbling plaster, mildew formation and so on. Careful attention to detailing is required to reduce the risk of thermal bridging.

Linear thermal transmittances and temperature factors should be calculated following the guidance set out in BR 497.[4] Reasonable provision would be to demonstrate that the specified details deliver a level of performance no worse than the standards set out in BRE IP 1/06.[5]

In addition, the builder would have to demonstrate that an appropriate system of site inspection is in place. Reasonable provision would be to:

(a)   adopt an **accredited construction details (ACDs)** approach (see Appendix 5.16 to this guide);

(b)   use the builder's own details, with the linear thermal transmittances calculated to BR 497[4] by a person with suitable expertise and experience – the values so calculated for linear thermal transmittance should be increased by 0.02W/m·K or 25% (whichever is the greater); or

(c)   use unaccredited details and apply a conservative default y-value of 0.15 in the DER calculation.

1.3.4   Ensure that air leakage details comply

Criterion 2: Limits on design flexibility

Air leakage can reduce the effectiveness of insulation and other energy conservation measures by up to 40%.

Air permeability is the physical property used to measure how airtight the building fabric is (AD L1A 3.1). The air permeability for new dwellings should be no worse than 10m³/h·m² at 50Pa (AD L1A, Table 2); however, it will probably be necessary to design for better performance than this in order to achieve a satisfactory DER.

Relying on an unusually high standard of airtightness to achieve a DER better than the TER also risks relying on an unusually high standard of workmanship, which will be tested at completion.

Guidance on appropriate air permeability standards for different ventilation strategies can be found in GPG 268.[6] Higher standards of airtightness are required for whole-house mechanical ventilation systems than for local extract systems with background ventilation.

Please refer to Appendix 5.8 of this guide.

1.3.5 Specify efficient boilers, pipework and controls

Criterion 2: Limits on design flexibility

Each fixed building service should be at least as efficient as the worst acceptable value for each appliance as set out in the *Domestic Building Services Compliance Guide*.[7] This covers heating system efficiency for various heating systems, fuels including renewable energy and community heating schemes, insulation of distribution pipework/ductwork, controls, installation and commissioning.

Boiler efficiency is not a constant and varies according to the season of the year and the varying loads placed on the boiler. A standard of assessing seasonal efficiency of gas and oil appropriate to the UK has been devised and is known as the SEDBUK (seasonal efficiency of domestic boilers in the UK) method. All new gas and oil boilers are rated by independently certified testing and placed on the boiler efficiency database at http://www.boilers.org.uk. The list is updated monthly.

To meet the CO_2 emission targets, it will help if primary pipe/duct runs are kept to a minimum, wet circuits are fully pumped and pipes/ducts are well insulated. Controls such as boiler interlock, thermostatic radiator valves and cylinder and room thermostats should limit the time the boiler is running to the minimum, and this is reflected in SAP calculations.

Please refer to Appendices 5.9, 5.10 and 5.11 for details.

1.3.6 Specify energy-efficient lighting

Criterion 2: Limits on design flexibility

Reasonable provision for energy-efficient lighting is given in the *Domestic Building Services Compliance Guide*.[7]

It will generally be adequate to provide a low-energy light fitting in no fewer than three out of every four light fittings in each of the main dwelling spaces. Low-energy light fittings should have a luminous efficacy of greater than 45 lamp-lumens/circuit-watt (see p. 36). Infrequently accessed spaces (e.g. storage and other areas) are excluded from this requirement, as are light fittings with supplied power below 5 circuit-watts per fitting.

External lighting must have automatic daylight control and can have user control where lamp efficacy is greater than 45 lumens/circuit-watt, otherwise lamps must have a lamp capacity of no greater than 100 lamp-watts and be fitted with occupancy control.

1.3.7   Use of mechanical ventilation

Criterion 2: Limits on design flexibility

The performance criteria for mechanical ventilation are described in Part F of the Building Regulations.[8] The factors to be considered in Part L are the airtightness of the building and ductwork and the efficiency of fans. Natural ventilation is the most common means of providing ventilation, but external pollution and noise may preclude its use, and mechanical ventilation combined with heat recovery can significantly reduce overall energy use.

Simple extractor fans operated by humidistats or timers to keep running time to a minimum may be needed under Part F to remove condensation from kitchens and bathrooms, as well as odours from toilets. Part L requires that these, or any other ventilation system, should meet minimum standards and should be easy to control and maintain to keep them working efficiently.

Please refer to Appendix 5.12 for details.

1.3.8   Confirm that design is not subject to summer overheating

Criterion 3: Limiting the effects of solar gains in summer

As increased insulation has reduced heat demand, the risk of summer overheating has increased. Solar gain is the primary cause of external heat gain, but many causes are internal, for example from cooking and hot water systems, appliances, lighting and people.

In dwellings, provisions should be made for passive control measures to limit the effect of solar gains on indoor temperatures during summer, irrespective of whether or not the dwelling has mechanical cooling (AD L1A 3.27).

Solar gain is reduced by a combination of choosing an appropriate window size, orientation and shading, and by using high thermal capacity construction that can be cooled using night ventilation. SAP contains a procedure to enable designers to check whether solar gains are excessive.

Please refer to Appendix 5.7 for details.

1.3.9 Work out your actual emissions (dwelling emission rate)

Criterion 1: Achieving the TER

The above information should allow readers to calculate the actual dwelling CO_2 emissions. Two calculations are required, using the same calculation tool as for TER: the first, a preliminary calculation based on plans and specifications as part of the design submission to building control to identify the design features critical to energy performance; the other, a calculation made when the building is complete and air permeability test results are known or default values are applied (see 5.2.3).

Should the designer wish to use any energy-saving technology or solutions that are not included in the published SAP specification, the data must be available on the SAP website[1] (or a site linked to it). These must have been independently tested in accordance with the procedures set out in Appendix Q[9] of SAP 2009 and included in the report providing evidence of compliance.

Please refer to Appendix 5.2 for details.

1.3.10 Ensure that the dwelling emission rate is equal to or better than the target emission rate

Criterion 1: Achieving the TER

In order to achieve the TER, it may be necessary to achieve a design air permeability better than the limit value [10m³/h·m² at 50Pa], particularly when using balanced systems with heat recovery. Also, U-values may have to be significantly better than those limiting values listed in AD L1A, and a significant contribution to energy demand may need to be met by **LZC energy supply systems** – see Appendix 5.20.

Once air permeability test results are available, DER calculations should be carried out using the actual test results together with the performance criteria of all as-built elements, fittings and services. Please refer to 1.3.12 below and 5.4 for details.

1.3.11 Prescribe a system for site checking by an appropriate person

Criterion 4: Building performance consistent with DER

AD L1A 5.25 recommends that a commissioning plan should be prepared, identifying systems that need to be tested and tests that will be carried out, and provided with the design-stage TER/BER calculation. The *Model Commissioning Plan* (BSRIA BG 8/2009) sets out how this should be documented.

It is sensible to ensure that ongoing inspections take place so that the quality of the important energy-saving features of the design is not compromised by workmanship (air permeability, airtightness of ducting, quality of insulation installation, potential thermal bridges and condensation risks) – for example, by adopting ACDs before they are covered by subsequent construction.

Please refer to Appendices 5.16 and 5.17.

1.3.12 Undertake pressure testing during construction

Criterion 4: Building performance consistent with DER

As-built performance checks are likely to fail if the designer has not already taken air permeability into account in the design of the building (see 1.3.4).

The approved procedure, specifically the method that tests the building envelope for pressure testing, is given in the Air Tightness Testing and Measurement Association (**ATTMA**) publication *Measuring Air Permeability of Building Envelopes.*[10] The manner approved for recording the results and the data on which they are based is given in section 4 of that document.

For each development an air pressure test should be carried out on three units of each dwelling type or 50% of all instances of that dwelling type (whichever is less), selected by the BCB.

Please refer to Appendix 5.8 for details.

Where no more than two dwellings are erected on a development site, as an alternative to testing, reasonable provision would be:

(a)   to demonstrate that, during the preceding 12-month period, a dwelling of the same dwelling type constructed by the same builder had been pressure tested to achieve the design air permeability; or

(b)   to avoid the need for any pressure testing by using a value of 15m³/h·m² at 50Pa for the air permeability when calculating the DER.

For developments with several dwellings, a sample of dwellings should be tested. Guidance on the number of types of dwellings that should be tested is set out in AD L1A 5.18 and 5.19.

1.3.13 Prescribe remedial measures where testing fails

Criterion 4: Building performance consistent with DER

If a satisfactory performance is not achieved, then remedial measures should be carried out on the dwelling and new tests should be carried out until the dwelling achieves the required criteria. In addition, a further dwelling of the same dwelling type should be tested (AD L1A 5.21).

In addition to the remedial work on a dwelling that failed the initial test, other dwellings of the same dwelling type that have not been tested should be examined, and, where appropriate, similar remedial measures should be applied (AD L1A 5.22).

Although this will pass Part L, a poor airtightness result will appear on the EPC, which a vendor is required to provide to a purchaser, and this may affect the value of the building.

Please refer to Appendix 5.8 for further details.

1.3.14 Prescribe commissioning procedures and certification

Criterion 4: Building performance consistent with DER

Part L of the Building Regulations requires that fixed building services be commissioned by testing and adjustment as necessary to ensure that they use no more fuel and power than is reasonable.

A commissioning plan should be prepared with the design-stage TER/ DER calculation so that the BCB can check that commissioning is being undertaken as specified as the work proceeds.

Where a building notice or full plans have been given to a BCB, the notice of completion of commissioning should be given to that BCB within five days of completion.

For heating and hot water systems, the approved procedures are set out in the *Domestic Building Services Compliance Guide*.[7] For ventilation systems, an approved procedure would follow the guidance in the *Domestic Ventilation Compliance Guide*.[11]

Other than where controls are 'on' and 'off' switches, systems should be commissioned so that at completion the system(s) and their controls are left in working order and can be operated efficiently for the purpose of the conservation of fuel and power.

1.3.15 Provide an instruction manual for the fixed building services

Criterion 5: Provisions for energy-efficient operation of the dwelling

The owner of the dwelling should be provided with sufficient information about the building and its fixed building services so that the building can be operated using no more fuel and power than is reasonable.

A suitable set of operating and maintenance instructions should be provided that can be referred to over the service life of the system(s). These must be directly related to the particular systems installed in the dwelling and written in a way that householders can understand. This should include:

(a)   how to adjust time and temperature control settings; and
(b)   routine maintenance required for energy-efficient operation.

The data used to calculate the TER and the DER should be included in the logbook, and the occupier should be provided with the recommendations report generated with the EPC.

Please refer to Appendix 5.18 for details.

Notes

1.   *The Government's Standard Assessment Procedure for the Energy Rating of Dwellings* (SAP), see http://www.bre.co.uk/sap2009.
2.   BR 443 *Conventions for U-value Calculations*. BRE (2006).
3.   BRE Report BR 262 *Thermal Insulation: Avoiding Risks*. BRE (2001).
4.   BR 497 *Conventions for Calculating Linear Thermal Transmittance and Temperature Factors*. BRE (2007).
5.   BRE Information Paper IP 1/06 *Assessing the Effects of Thermal Bridging at Junctions and Around Openings* (2006).
6.   CE124/GPG 268 *Energy Efficient Ventilation in Housing. A Guide for Specifiers*. Energy Saving Trust (2006).
7.   *Domestic Building Services Compliance Guide*. CLG (2010).
8.   *Building Regulations Part F – Means of Ventilation*. CLG (2010).
9.   http://www.sap-appendixq.org.uk/page.jsp?id=1.
10.   *Measuring Air Permeability of Building Envelopes*. ATTMA (2006, due to be revised 2010).
11.   *Domestic Ventilation Compliance Guide*. CLG (2010).

AD L1B: existing dwellings

AD L1B *Conservation of Fuel and Power in Existing Dwellings* covers **extensions to a dwelling** (including **conservatories**) and **material alterations** to existing **dwellings**, as well as dwellings created by a **material change of use**. It also applies to work on certain services or fittings (called **controlled services** or **controlled fittings**) such as new external doors or windows, new hot water systems, mechanical ventilation and cooling systems, insulation of existing pipes and ducts, lighting or the provision of a new or changed **thermal element** (wall, roof or floor). Under certain circumstances, work in existing dwellings can trigger **consequential improvement works**.

2.1 Summary of 2010 changes to AD L1B

The main revisions to AD L1B made in 2010 are summarised below:

1. clearer distinctions made between the requirements of the Regulations and the guidance contained within the ADs;
2. standards defined for swimming pool basins in new dwellings (see 2.3.1 of this guide);
3. exemptions removed for conservatories with areas of less than 30m² in some cases (see 2.3.6 of this guide);
4. revised definition of renovation (see 2.3.5 of this guide); and
5. higher standards of performance generally.

2.2 The approaches and requirements vary with the nature of the work

The requirements vary and depend on whether you are providing an extension to an existing dwelling, adding a conservatory, changing the use of the building or making material alterations, or whether you are modifying an existing thermal element or a service. Table 2 shows the requirements for each of the possible approaches.

> The general rules of thumb for walls, floors and roofs are as follows:
>
> - where there is a new construction (e.g. to form an extension), or an element is being replaced, the standards set out in Table 2 of AD L1B for new thermal elements apply (AD L1B 5.2–5.4);
> - where an element or fitting is being renovated, the standards set out in Table 3, column (b), of AD L1B apply to the whole element wherever feasible (AD L1B 5.7–5.10); and
> - where an existing element becomes a thermal element the standards set out in Table 3, column (b), of AD L1B apply where the existing performance is worse than set out in Table 3, column (a) (AD L1B 5.11–5.13).

2.3 Compliance for work to existing dwellings

The broad requirements and the different methods of meeting them are listed in Table 2.

Table 2
The broad requirements for existing dwellings and how to meet them

Extension – there are three ways to comply with Part L1B if building an extension

Brief definition	An extension has an element of new-build construction required to enlarge an existing dwelling
Option 1	Areas of openings comply (AD L1B 4.2)
	AND
	U-values of openings (controlled fittings) comply with AD L1B 4.1b and Table 1
	AND
	Heating, hot water, pipes, mechanical ventilation, cooling and fixed internal and external lighting (controlled services) comply and are commissioned for efficient operation (AD L1B 4.3)
	AND
	New thermal elements to comply with standards set out in Table 2 for new elements in an extension (AD L1B 4.1a)

Table 2
Continued

Option 1 (cont.)	AND
	As few thermal bridges as possible (AD L1B 5.5 and 5.6)
	AND
	Reduction of unwanted air leakage (AD L1B 5.5 and 5.6)
	AND
	Existing fabric to meet requirements when it becomes a thermal element subject to simple payback calculation (AD L1B 5.7–5.13)
Option 2	Area-weighted U-value complies (AD L1B 4.5)
Option 3	Show that CO_2 emission for the actual dwelling plus the actual extension is better than the actual dwelling plus a notional extension complying with the standards of Option 1 using SAP (AD L1B 4.6 and 4.7)
Conservatories	
Brief definitions	Regulations do not apply to conservatories with a floor area of less than 30m² where the existing external fabric separating the dwelling from the conservatory is retained (or replaced to at least an equivalent standard)
	AND
	Where the heating system of the dwelling is not extended to the conservatory (AD L1B 3.15)
Reasonable provision	Thermally separated from attached building by fabric and fittings with U-value and draught-stripping provisions no worse than provided elsewhere in the building (AD L1B 4.8a)
	AND
	Any heating system to comply with the requirements of the *Domestic Building Services Compliance Guide*[1] and include independent temperature and on/off controls (AD L1B 4.8b)
	AND
	U-values of controlled fittings and thermal elements to be no worse than AD L1B Table 1 and Table 2 (AD L1B 4.8c)
	AND
	Commission fixed building services (AD L1B 4.30)
	AND
	Provide information that demonstrates that the conservatory satisfies these requirements (AD L1B Section 7)

Table 2
Continued

Material changes of use to become a dwelling or changes of energy status – two ways to comply: Options 1 and 2

Brief definition	This applies in the case when a building or a part of a building (even a room) becomes a dwelling. Also, if the number of dwellings changes or the number of rooms used as dwellings changes
Option 1	Where windows or doors (controlled fittings) are being provided or extended, or where they are being retained and their performance is worse than $3.3W/m^2{\cdot}K$, these should be as AD L1B Table 1 and have insulated cavity closers fitted. Total area of openings should generally be no more than 25% of the floor area
	AND
	Heating, hot water, pipes, mechanical ventilation, cooling, fixed internal and external lighting (controlled services) to comply and to be commissioned for efficient operation
	AND
	New thermal elements shall be to AD L1A Table 2 with provision for continuity of insulation and airtightness (AD L1B 4.15b)
	AND
	Renovated thermal elements to AD L1B Table 3, column (b), if their performance is worse than set out in column (a) (AD L1B 4.15c)
Option 2	Model the dwelling using SAP to show that the emissions from the proposed dwelling are no greater than if constructed to meet the requirements of Option 1 above (AD L1B 4.16)

Changes to controlled fittings

Brief definition	Controlled fittings are windows, roof windows, roof lights and doors
Reasonable provision	These should be as AD L1B Table 1 and insulated cavity closers should be fitted. Total area of openings should generally be no more than 25% of the floor area (AD L1B 4.19)

Changes to controlled services

Brief definition	Controlled services are heating and hot water systems, pipes and ducts, mechanical ventilation or cooling, fixed internal and dwelling-supplied external lighting and renewable or other LZC energy supply systems
Reasonable provision	Controlled services to comply with the *Domestic Building Services Compliance Guide*[1] and to be commissioned for efficient operation (AD L1B 4.24)

Table 2
Continued

Changes to thermal element

Brief definition	A thermal element is a wall, floor or roof that separates internal conditioned spaces from the external environment
New, in an extension	New thermal elements to AD L1B Table 2 with provision for continuity of insulation and airtightness (AD L1B 5.5 and 5.6)
Renovated, change that amends thermal performance such as adding new insulation layer	To the standards set out in AD L1B Table 3, column (b), if their performance is worse than set out in column (a) subject to feasibility and a simple payback period of 15 years OR (If the above is not technically feasible) upgrade to the best standard that is technically feasible with a simple payback period of 15 years (AD L1B 5.7–5.10)
Retained, either where the building is subject to a material change of use or where an existing element becomes part of the thermal envelope (e.g. loft or garage conversion)	To the standards set out in AD L1B Table 3, column (b), if their performance is worse than set out in column (a) subject to feasibility and a simple payback period of 15 years OR (If the above is not technically feasible) upgrade to the best standard that is technically feasible with a simple payback period of 15 years (AD L1B 5.11–5.13)

Note that specific guidance applies to **historic buildings**, including listed buildings, buildings that are referred to in the local authority's development plan as being of local architectural or historic interest and those buildings in national parks, areas of outstanding natural beauty and world heritage sites (AD L1B 3.6). When dealing with a historic building, the aim should be to improve energy efficiency as far as is reasonably practical without prejudicing the character of the building or risking long-term deterioration. Specific guidance is available from English Heritage.[2]

Which road map to follow depends on the specific nature of the work to be done, and this is best resolved using either Table 2 or the flowchart shown in Figure 2. When it is known which requirements apply, a brief explanation in the following text can be found or, if required, there is a more detailed explanation in the appendices.

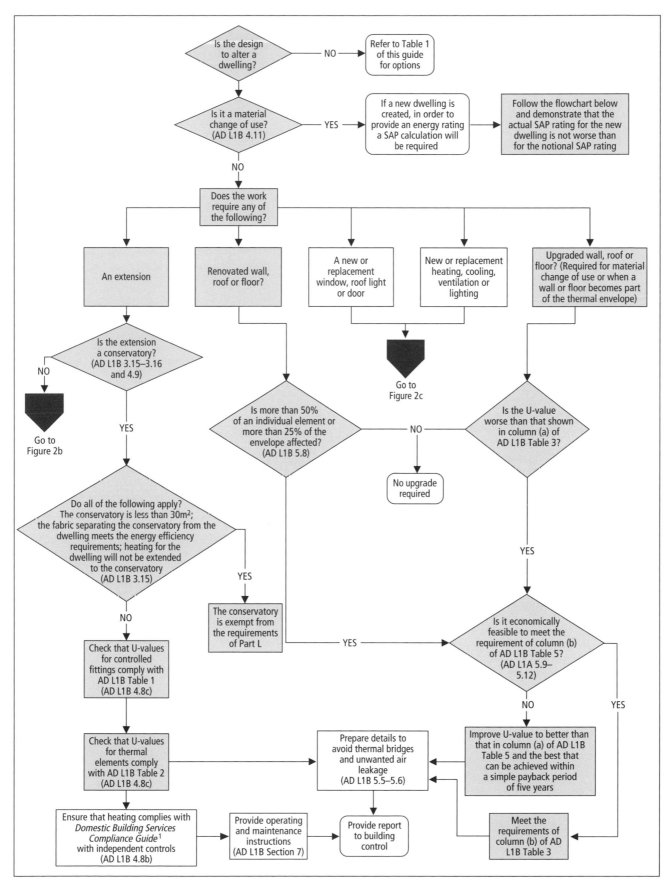

Figure 2a
AD L1B existing dwelling

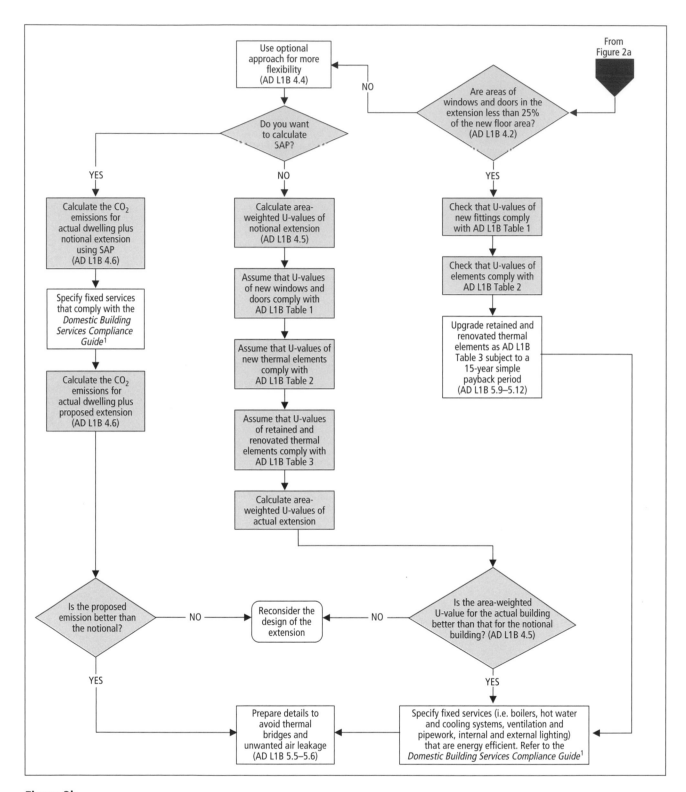

Figure 2b
AD L1B existing dwelling (extension)

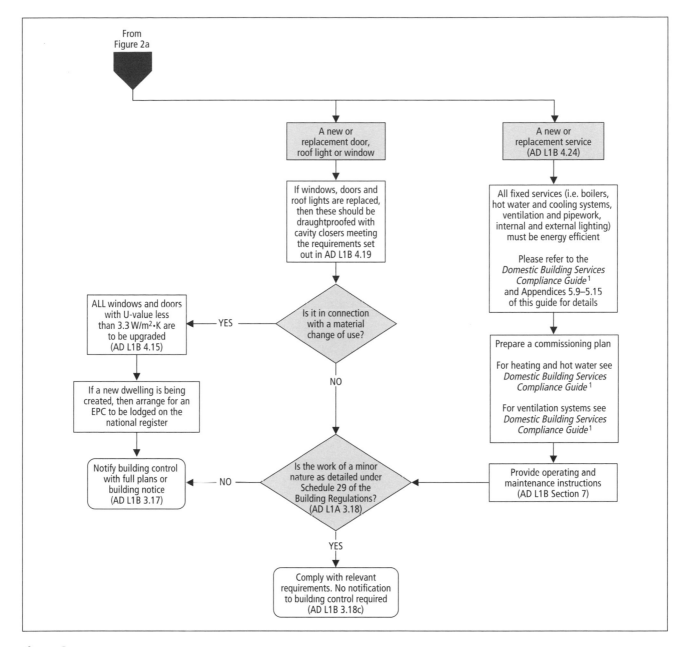

Figure 2c
Existing dwelling (controlled fittings and services)

Note that increasing insulation or introducing other energy efficiency measures into an existing building can increase technical risks, particularly of condensation formation, because of either thermal bridging or interstitial condensation where this did not occur before the works. General guidance on technical risk relating to insulation improvements is contained in BR 262.[3]

2.3.1 Fabric standards – ensure that U-values and areas of openings comply

Applies to extensions (Table 2, Option 1) and material change of use (Table 2, Option 1).

This is the simplest, but least flexible, approach to achieving the required thermal performance when designing an extension (AD L1B 5.2–5.13).

New thermal elements (i.e. walls, roofs, floors, swimming pool basins) should meet the standards set out in AD L1B Table 2. Where thermal elements are renovated, they should meet the standards set out in column (b) of AD L1B Table 3 wherever feasible and where such improvements achieve a simple payback period of 15 years or less. Where thermal elements are retained and their U-value is worse than the threshold value set out in column (a) of AD L1B Table 3, they should be upgraded to achieve the standards set out in column (b) wherever feasible and subject to achieving a simple payback period of 15 years or less.

The U-values of new and replacement windows and doors should each meet one of the requirements of AD L1B Table 1. For extensions, the total area of openings is limited to 25% of the floor area *plus* the areas of openings blocked up as a result of extension works. If the glazed area is less than 20% of the floor area, parts of the extension may experience poor levels of daylight. For material changes of use, all windows with a U-value of less than 3.3W/m^2·K should be replaced to the standards set out in AD L1B Table 1 and openings limited to 25% of the floor area (AD L1B 4.2).

All U-values should be calculated to BR 443.[4]

2.3.2 Fabric standards – show compliance using the area-weighted U-value calculation

Available as an alternative approach to 2.3.1 above where more flexibility is required when designing extensions (Table 2, Option 2).

The AD allows some flexibility (AD L1B 4.5) where it can be shown that the area-weighted U-value of all the elements in the extension is no greater than that of an extension of the same size and shape that complies with standards for thermal elements and openings set out in 2.3.1 above.

The area-weighted U-value is give by the following expression:

$$[(U1 \times A1) + (U2 \times A2) + (U3 \times A3) + ...] \div (A1 + A2 + A3 + ...)$$

2.3.3 Fabric standards – confirm that thermal bridges are compliant and air leakage is reduced

The following applies wherever the thermal performance of an element or fitting has been improved.

The building should be constructed so that there is no unwanted air leakage through the new envelope parts or thermal bridges in the insulation layers caused by gaps within the various elements, gaps in the joints between elements and gaps at the edges of elements such as those around window and door openings.

A suitable approach to showing that the requirement has been achieved would be to provide insulated cavity closers in all openings and to adopt **ACDs** for other junctions.

Please refer to Appendices 5.2, 5.8 and 5.16 for details.

2.3.4 Fabric standards – show compliance using Standard Assessment Procedure modelling (whole-dwelling calculation method)

Available as another alternative approach if even more design flexibility is required for extensions (Option 3) or as the method of compliance for significantly glazed extensions and as an option for a material change of use (Option 2) or material alterations.

SAP can be used to demonstrate that the total emissions from the extension/modified dwelling are no greater than those for a notional dwelling of the same size and shape as the proposed dwelling designed to the above standards. The reference standards are as follows:

- extensions: fabric to AD L1B 4.1, controlled fittings to AD L1B 4.2, controlled services to AD L1B 4.3;
- material change of use: to the standards set out in AD L1B 4.11;
- change in energy status (e.g. owing to material alteration): to the standards set out in AD L1B 4.12–4.15.

Please refer to Appendix 5.4 for details on SAP calculations in general.

2.3.5 Justify reduced standards using the 15-year payback criterion

The following applies wherever existing elements are retained but need to be either renovated or upgraded because they are part of an extension (Option 1) or because they are part of a material change of use, change in energy status (Option 1) or a material alteration.

> Payback is applicable only when renovating an existing element or where improvements are required for an existing element that becomes a thermal element (e.g. where an existing garage is converted to occupied accommodation).
>
> Renovation is defined as the provision of a new layer through either of the following activities:
>
> (a) providing new layers by:
>   i.   cladding or rendering the external surface of the thermal element; or
>   ii. dry-lining the internal surface of a thermal element.
>
> (b) replacing existing layers by:
>   i.   stripping down an element to expose the structure and then rebuilding to meet performance requirements; or
>   ii. replacing the waterproof membrane of a flat roof.

When extending a building or renewing or refurbishing a thermal element (wall, roof or floor), there may be situations when full compliance with an upgrade of the U-value is not viable because of economic, functional or technical difficulties.

Please refer to Appendix 5.29 for details on how to calculate simple payback.

2.3.6 Confirm that conservatories comply with requirements

The following applies to conservatories other than those with a floor area of less than 30m² where the existing walls, doors and windows in the part of the dwelling that separates the conservatory are retained (or, if removed, replaced by walls, doors and windows that meet the energy efficiency requirements) and where the heating system of the dwelling is not extended to the conservatory.

The requirements for conservatories are set out in AD L1B 4.8 and 4.9.

For conservatories:

(a) Thermal separation between the heated area of the conservatory and the existing dwelling should be insulated and draughtproofed to at least the same extent as the existing dwelling.

(b) Glazed elements should comply with the standards set out in AD L1B Table 1 and thermal elements should have U-values no worse than those in Table 2 (general limitations on total area of glazing and doors set out in AD L1B 4.2 do not apply).

(c) If a heating system is provided, that system should comply with the minimum standards in the *Domestic Building Services Compliance Guide*[1] (with automatic controls such that conservatory heating need not default to the same schedule as the main house).

The person responsible for constructing the conservatory should provide the owner with a schedule that demonstrates that the conservatory satisfies these requirements and is thermally separated from the rest of the dwelling.

2.3.7 Specify efficient boilers, pipework and controls

The following applies wherever fixed building services are being installed, extended or replaced. When replacing an existing appliance, the efficiency of the new appliance must not be significantly less than the original equipment and the carbon intensity should be considered when fuels are changed.

The standards required for the following services are set out in the *Domestic Building Services Compliance Guide*[1]:

- heating and hot water systems (including insulation of pipes, ducts and vessels;
- mechanical ventilation; and
- mechanical cooling/air conditioning.

If a particular technology is not covered in the *Domestic Building Services Compliance Guide*,[1] **reasonable provision** and then comparison should be made by reference to a system of the same type for which details are given in the guide.

Please refer to Appendix 5.9 of this guide for information about efficient boilers.

Zone controls are required for replacement heating systems in all dwellings other than those that are single storey and open plan. Separate time and temperature controls for the hot water cylinder are not required when only the hot water cylinder is being replaced in an existing system that does not have separate controls.

Accessible pipes should be insulated to the same standards as new dwellings unless there are practical constraints.

2.3.8 Specify energy-efficient lighting

Reasonable provision for energy-efficient lighting is given in the *Domestic Building Services Compliance Guide*.[1]

It will generally be adequate to provide a low-energy light fitting in at least three out of every four light fittings in each of the main dwelling spaces. Low-energy light fittings should have a luminous efficacy of greater than 45 lamp-lumens/circuit-watt. Infrequently accessed spaces (e.g. storage and other areas) are excluded from this requirement, as are light fittings with supplied power below 5 circuit-watts per fitting.

External lighting must have automatic daylight control and can have user control where lamp efficacy is greater than 45 lumens/circuit-watt, otherwise lamps must have a lamp capacity of no greater than 100 lamp-watts and be fitted with occupancy control.

2.3.9 Commissioning procedures

Part L of the Building Regulations requires that fixed building services are to be commissioned by testing and adjustment as necessary to ensure that they use no more fuel and power than is reasonable.

Where a building notice or full plans have been given to a BCB, the notice of completion of commissioning should be given to that BCB within five days of completing the commissioning.

For heating and hot water systems, the approved procedures are set out in the *Domestic Building Services Compliance Guide*.[1] For ventilation systems, an approved procedure would to follow the guidance in the *Domestic Ventilation Compliance Guide*.[5]

Other than where controls are 'on' and 'off' switches, systems should be commissioned so that, at completion, the system(s) and their controls are left in working order and can be operated efficiently for the purpose of conservation of fuel and power.

2.3.10 Provide an instruction manual for the fixed building services

The owner of the dwelling should be provided with sufficient information about the building and its fixed building services so that it can be operated using no more fuel and power than is reasonable.

A suitable set of operating and maintenance instructions should be provided, which can be referred to over the service life of the system(s). This must be directly related to the particular systems installed in the dwelling and written in a way that householders can understand. This should include information on:

(a)   how to adjust time and temperature control settings; and
(b)   routine maintenance required for energy-efficient operation.

Please refer to Appendix 5.18 for details.

2.3.11 Consequential improvements

Regulation 17D of the Building Regulations may require additional work (consequential improvement works) to improve the energy efficiency of existing buildings where certain types of work are proposed. These affect dwellings with a total **useful floor area** greater than 1000m^2 where the proposed work consists of:

(a)   an extension;
(b)   the initial provision of any fixed building service (other than a renewable energy generator);
(c)   an increase to the installed capacity of any fixed building service.

There are a relatively small number of existing dwellings that are greater than 1000m^2 and the guidance for achieving compliance is contained within AD L2B (see 4.3.1 of this guide).

Notes

1.   *Domestic Building Services Compliance Guide.* CLG (2010).
2.   *Building Regulations and Historic Buildings.* English Heritage (2002, revised 2004).
3.   BRE Report BR 262 *Thermal Insulation: Avoiding Risks.* BRE (2001).
4.   BR 443 *Conventions for U-value Calculations.* BRE (2006).
5.   *Domestic Ventilation Compliance Guide.* CLG (2010).

AD L2A: new buildings other than dwellings

AD L2A *Conservation of Fuel and Power in New Buildings other than Dwellings* covers new buildings other than **dwellings** and includes the first **fit-out works** to a building. This part covers heated common areas in residential buildings as well as nursing homes, student accommodation and, in mixed-use developments, the commercial or retail space. It also includes extensions of areas greater than 100m^2 and greater than 25% of the existing floor area.

3.1 Summary of 2010 changes to AD L2A

The main revisions to AD L2A made in 2010 are summarised below:

1. Criterion 1: The most significant change between 2006 and 2010 is a change to the basis of the notional building used to determine the **TER**: a 2010 notional building is now used for calculating the TER. The new methodology is referred to as the 'aggregate 25% approach'. The revised version of the national calculation methodology (NCM) provides guidance on the use of the Simplified Building Energy Model (SBEM) and other approved software tools using the 'aggregate 25% approach' (see 3.3.1 and 5.1 of this guide). Criterion 1 also requires a design-stage TER/**BER** calculation as a means of helping to improve compliance.

2. Criterion 2: The *Non-domestic Building Services Compliance Guide*[1] replaces the *Non-domestic Heating, Cooling and Ventilation Compliance Guide*. The new guide includes additional sections on wind-powered electricity generating systems, solar photovoltaic systems, lighting, heating system glandless circulators and water pumps.

3. Criterion 3: The procedure for demonstrating that **reasonable provision** has been made to limit the effects of solar gain in summer has been revised (see 3.3.7 of this guide).

4. Criterion 4: A commissioning plan should be drawn up and submitted at the design stage, so that building control can check that commissioning is being done as work proceeds (see 3.3.13 of this guide).

5. Criterion 5: A recommendations report is required to inform the occupier how the energy performance of the building might be further improved.

3.2   The five criteria

All five criteria have to be met without compromising the other requirements of the Building Regulations.

The criteria are:

1. The predicted CO_2 emission rate for the building as constructed (the BER) must not be greater than the TER.
2. The performance of the building fabric, heating, hot water and fixed lighting systems should achieve reasonable overall standards of energy efficiency.
3. The building has appropriate passive control measures to limit solar gains.
4. The performance of the building, as built, should be consistent with the prediction made in the BER.
5. The necessary provisions for enabling energy-efficient operation should be put in place.

3.3   A simple road map for compliance

By following this map the user will be able to determine how to meet the requirements of Part L of the Building Regulations for new buildings other than dwellings. The broad principles are to:

1. reduce energy demand;
2. meet remaining energy demands with high-efficiency systems;
3. use low-carbon energy supplies and systems;
4. provide operating instructions and monitoring facilities so that occupants can manage their energy use; and
5. meet the necessary provisions for enabling energy-efficient operation of the building, such as commissioning procedures and provision over user instruction manuals.

3.3.1 Work out the target emission rate

The TER is expressed as the amount of CO_2 in kilograms emitted per square metre of floor area per year as the result of the provision of heating, hot water, lighting, and ventilation and cooling, and assuming a notional building (described in the 2010 NCM) and a selection of 'standardised activities' when assessed by an **approved calculation tool**. 'Standardised activities' have associated default standards for occupancy times and environmental conditions (temperature, illumination, ventilation rate, etc.). The approved calculation tool is either SBEM or other approved software (as set out in the *Notice of Approval of the Methodology of Calculation of the Energy Performance of Buildings in England and Wales*).[2]

The TER is the result of the calculation of CO_2 emissions from heating, hot water, cooling, auxiliary energy, ventilation and lighting in a 2010 notional building with default properties as described in paragraphs 19–66 of the 2010 *NCM Modelling Guide*[3] (details of the information required and how this is actually done are included in Appendix 5.1 of this guide).

Providing the building satisfies the limits on design flexibility, as set out in Criterion 2, there is an opportunity to use LZC energy sources, for example solar hot water and photovoltaic power [such as those described in *Low or Zero Carbon Energy Sources – Strategic Guide,*[4] available on the Department of Communities and Local Government (DCLG) website at http://www.dclg.gov.uk]; however, the opportunity to trade this off against other requirements is limited (paragraphs 4.18–4.18c of Part L2A).

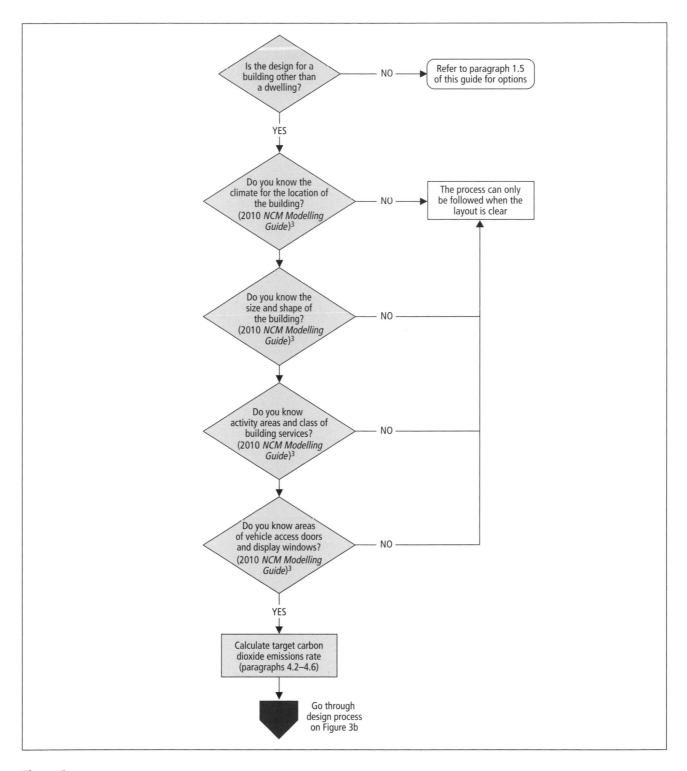

Figure 3a
Road map for meeting the provisions of Part L2A: calculating the TER

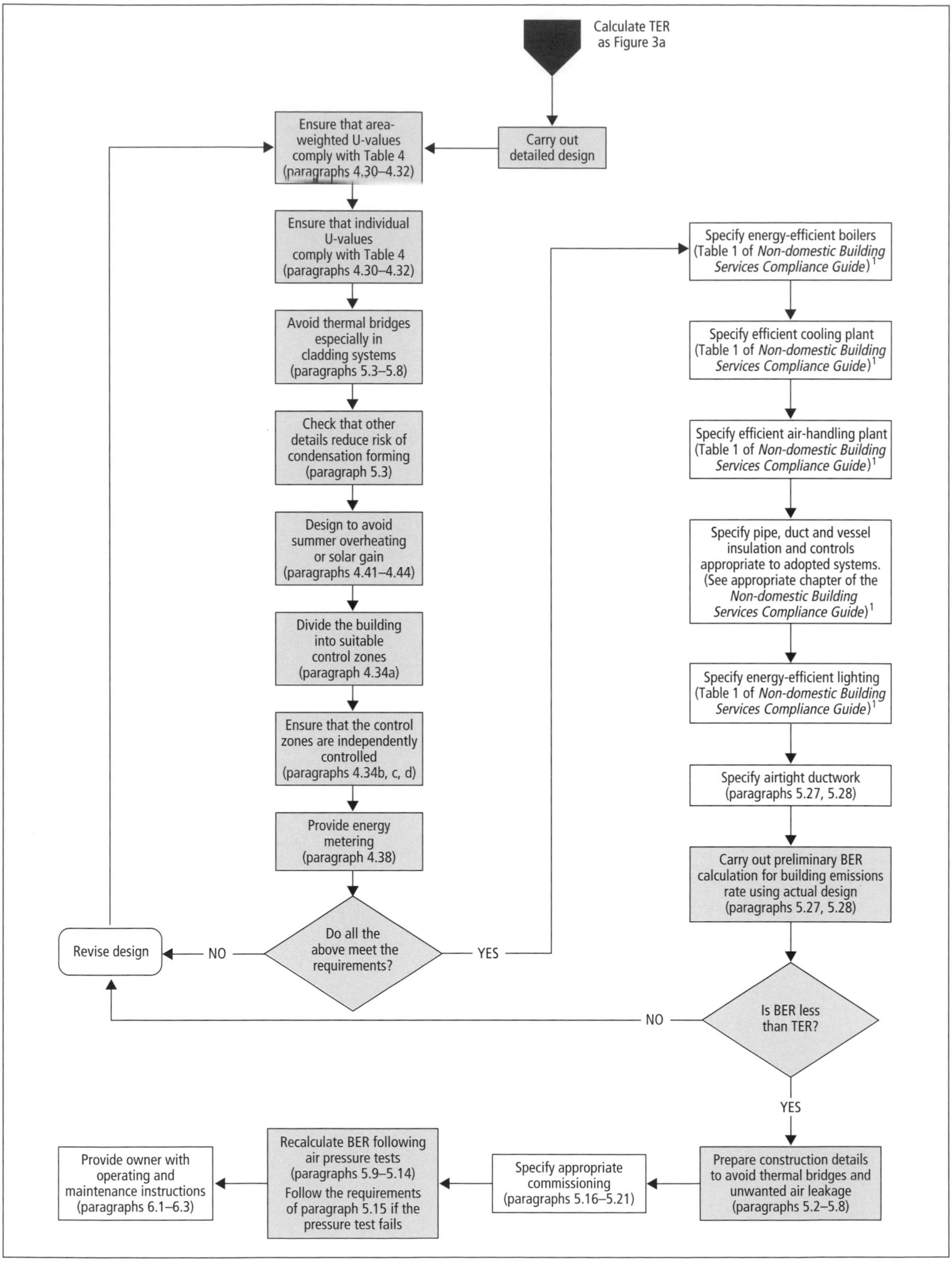

Figure 3b
Road map for meeting the provisions of Part L2A: design process

3.3.2   Ensure that U-values comply

Criterion 2: Limits on design flexibility

AD L2A Table 4 gives U-values for limiting fabric parameters.

It is important to check that all U-values in the design meet these minimum levels; however, it is likely that these U-values will have to be improved in order to meet the TER.

It is also important to check details and calculations to rule out the risk of interstitial condensation (BR 262).[5]

Please refer to Appendix 5.6 for details of U-values.

3.3.3   Check for condensation risk in curtain walling and cladding

Criterion 2: Limits on design flexibility

There are a number of ways in which Part L encourages the use of low-carbon equipment without going so far as to insist on it. For example, in general, where heating systems are capable of being fired by more than one fuel, the fuel with the highest CO_2 emission factor should be used to calculate the BER. However, where biomass heating is used with supplementary heating from an alternative fuel, in some circumstances the BER **can** be calculated as a weighted average for the two fuels based on the anticipated usage (AD L2A 4.16).

It is important to check details and calculations to rule out the risk of interstitial or surface condensation.

The support structures for curtain walling and cladding systems often form pathways for heat loss through the system. They need to be carefully detailed to avoid thermal bridging as well as to avoid overall worsening of U-value performance. Manufacturers should be able to provide computer-generated calculations to demonstrate adequate performance of key details such as corners, junctions, protrusions, edges and at points of structural support.

Please refer to Appendix 5.6 for details of U-values.

3.3.4 Ensure that air leakage details comply

Criterion 2: Limits on design flexibility

Air leakage reduces the effectiveness of insulation and other energy conservation measures by up to 40%.

Air permeability is the physical property used to measure the air tightness of the building fabric (AD L2A 5.9–5.15). The design air permeability used in the TER calculation is 10m³/h·m² at 50Pa (AD L2A 5.14a); however, it will probably be necessary to design for better performance than this to achieve a satisfactory BER, particularly in buildings with mechanical ventilation and air conditioning.

Please refer to Appendix 5.2.3 of this guide for ways of improving the **DER**.

Please refer to Appendix 5.8 for details.

3.3.5 Specify efficient boilers, chillers, pipework, ductwork and controls

Criterion 2: Limits on design flexibility

Not subject to Part L are emergency escape lighting and specialist process lighting (such as theatre spotlights, projection equipment, TV and photographic studio lighting, medical lighting in operating theatres and doctors' and dentists' surgeries, illuminated signs, coloured or stroboscopic lighting and art objects with integral lighting such as sculptures, decorative fountains and chandeliers).

Two units have been used: luminaire-lumens/circuit-watt and lamp-lumens/circuit-watt. A luminaire contains one or more lamps housed in a fitting, and care must be taken to ensure that the correct units are being applied.

Please refer to the *Non-domestic Building Services Compliance Guide*.[1] This sets out clear guidance on means of complying with AD L2A, and has sections on boilers, heat pumps, gas- and oil-fired warm air heaters, gas- and oil-fired radiant technology, combined heat and power (CHP), electric space heating, domestic-scale hot water, comfort cooling, air distribution systems, pipework and duct insulation, wind-powered electricity-generating systems, solar photovoltaic systems, lighting, heating system glandless circulators and water pumps. The guide also includes a compliance checklist and a tool for data input into the NCM.

The guide sets out the minimum provisions for:

- the efficiency of the plant that generates heat, hot water or cooling;
- controls to ensure no unnecessary or excessive use of the systems;
- other factors affecting the safety or energy efficiency of the system;
- the insulation of pipes and ducts; and
- acceptable specific fan power ratings for fans serving air distribution systems.

In addition, there is a set of non-prescriptive additional measures to improve plant efficiency.

The data are provided in a way that is consistent with the NCM used by the SBEM.

Please refer to Appendices 5.9– 5.11 for details.

3.3.6   Provide for energy metering

Criterion 2: Limits on design flexibility

AD L2A acknowledges that properly planned plant control and energy-metering equipment can contribute substantially to the energy performance of the building. This means thinking of the building in terms of zones with similar energy control requirements (owing to exposure or use) and giving those zones independent control of timing, temperature and ventilation. AD L2A 4.28–4.39 describes a reasonable provision for energy metering that includes assigning energy consumption to use, providing separate meters for monitoring LZC emission systems and including automatic meter readings and data collection for buildings with an area greater than 1000m^2.

AD L2A 4.16 allows the BER to be reduced by a factor of 5% through the use of automatic monitoring and targeting, with alarms for out-of-range values where this is achieved through a complete installation that measures, records, transmits, analyses, reports and communicates meaningful energy management information to enable the operator to manage the energy it uses.

3.3.7   Confirm that lighting is suitably efficient

Criterion 2: Limits on design flexibility

Please refer to the *Non-domestic Building Services Compliance Guide*.[1] Section 12 provides guidance on specifying lighting for new and existing buildings to meet the minimum energy efficiency standards in the Building Regulations.

Table 44 of the above sets out minimum lighting efficacy in new buildings in terms of general lighting and display lighting.

Table 47 of the above sets out standards for lighting controls for general and display lighting in new and existing buildings.

Please refer to Appendix 5.14 for details.

3.3.8   Confirm that the design is not subject to summer overheating

Criterion 3: Limiting the effects of solar gain in summer

Although solar gain is the primary cause of external heat gain, there are also internal causes such as lighting, electronic equipment (including computers) and, in all cases, human beings.

AD L2A 4.41–4.44 requires that provision should be made to limit solar gain in occupied spaces.

Please refer to Appendix 5.7 for details.

3.3.9   Work out the building emission rate

Criterion 1: Achieving the TER

Two calculations are required to demonstrate that the BER of the building, both as designed and after completion, is not greater than the TER (automatically calculated by the same tool used to calculate the energy performance of the actual building). Under paragraph 4.11, a preliminary calculation is required prior to construction. This design-stage submission of the first calculation will assist the BCB by identifying critical features of the design that will affect the energy performance of the building so that these can be monitored through the construction process. The second calculation and final submission is made when the building is complete.

It takes into account any changes in specification and the actual results of the air permeability, ductwork leakage and fan performance tests.

Please refer to Appendix 5.3 for more details.

3.3.10 Ensure that the building emission rate is equal to or better than the target emission rate

Criterion 1: Achieving the TER

This comparison is done within SBEM or any of the other approved software tools. Please see Appendix 5.5 for details of how to generate this comparison through SBEM.

There is an opportunity in Part L2A to adjust the BER to take advantage of enhanced management and control procedures to improve energy conservation (see Table 2 for power factor adjustments for enhanced management and control features).

Please refer to Appendix 5.3 for details.

3.3.11 Prescribe a system for site checking by a qualified inspector

Criterion 4: Quality of construction and commissioning

AD L2A 5.17 recommends that a commissioning plan should be prepared that identifies systems that need to be tested and the tests that will be carried out by a **qualified inspector**, and it should be provided with the design-stage TER/BER calculation.

It is sensible to ensure that ongoing inspections take place so that the quality of the important energy-saving features of the design is not compromised by poor workmanship (air permeability, airtightness of ducting, quality of insulation installation, and potential thermal bridges and condensation risks) – for example, by adopting **ACDs** before they are covered by subsequent construction.

Please refer to Appendices 5.16 and 5.17 for details.

3.3.12 Undertake fabric leakage and ductwork leakage tests

Criterion 4: Quality of construction and commissioning

There are a number of cases in which air testing may not be required (AD L2A 5.13), for example:

An alternative to testing for buildings with a floor area less than 500m^2 is to assume an air permeability of 15m^3/h·m^2; this will require increasing the performance of the building in other aspects to meet the TER.

Prefabricated buildings with no site assembly may not require testing, provided that routine site-based testing on that module type has been successfully carried out in the past by a third party accredited inspector.

In the case of large extensions, where sealing off the extension is impractical, the approach to air testing should be agreed with the BCB.

In the case of large complex buildings, where it can be shown and endorsed by an **approved competent person** that pressure testing is impractical using the guidance in the **ATTMA** publication, an air permeability of no less than 5.0m^3/h·m^2 at 50Pa can be assumed. However, this assumption can only be made if a **suitably qualified person** has carried out the following:

(a)   a programme of design detail development:
     i   component testing to show that design air permeability has been achieved;
     ii   site supervision; and
(b)   a demonstration that a complete air barrier around the whole building envelope will be achieved.

For buildings that are divided into self-contained units, representative tests would be reasonable.

Where pressure testing is undertaken, it shall be assessed using the method to test the building envelope as set out in *Measuring Air Permeability of Building Envelopes*,[6] with results recorded as set out in Section 4 of that same document. As-built performance checks are likely to fail if the designer has not already taken the airtightness of fabric and ducts into account in the design of the building (see 3.3.4 above).

Please refer to Appendix 5.8 for more details.

Ductwork on systems served by fans with a design flow rate greater than 1m³/s (and also ducts designed for the BER to have leak rates lower than standard) should be tested for leakage (AD L2A 5.27) by a suitably competent person [e.g. a member of the Heating and Ventilation Contractors Association (HVCA) specialist ductwork group or a member of the Association of Ductwork Contractors and Allied Services] in accordance with procedures set out in the HVCA DW 143.[7]

3.3.13 Prescribe remedial measures where testing fails

Criterion 4: Quality of construction and commissioning

It would be useful to prepare a commissioning plan at the design stage (AD L2A 5.17).

In most cases, remedial measures will involve the use of sealants and/or expanding foam fillers unless there are obvious missing draught seals or membranes that can be readily replaced.

If a test result shows that leakage is higher than anticipated, it is recommended that suspect details are selectively blanked off temporarily and the test re-run. This should give valuable information with regard to the design of remedial measures. A list of vulnerable locations is given in Appendix 5.8.

If a building fails to achieve its design air permeability, it may still meet the requirements if it achieves both the target air permeability and BER. A construction failing on both of these criteria must be retested following the implementation of remedial measures.

If there is a test failure on a representative area of a building compartmentalised into self-contained units as described in AD L2A 5.13e, then after remedial work another representative area should also be tested.

If ductwork fails the leakage tests, carry out remedial work and retesting of new sections as set out in DW 143.[7]

3.3.14 Confirm that the building emission rate is equal to or better than the target emission rate as constructed

Criterion 1: Achieving the TER

Once air permeability test results are available, BER calculations should be carried out using the actual test results together with the performance criteria of all as-built elements, fittings and services. Please also refer to 3.3.13 above.

3.3.15 Prescribe commissioning procedures and certification

Criterion 5: Operating and maintenance instructions

New buildings and works to existing buildings will require commissioning of all **controlled services** (heating, hot water, electrical and mechanical) in accordance with Chartered Institute of Building Services Engineers (CIBSE) Code M[8] by a **commissioning specialist** (individual or organisation) from the Commissioning Specialists Association or the commissioning group of the HVCA.

Note also the requirement for ductwork testing in 3.3.12 above.

AD L2A 6.2 and 6.3 requires the preparation of a logbook. The logbook should be suitable for day-to-day use and [if only by summary reference to operating and maintenance manuals or to the Construction Design and Management (CDM) Health And Safety File] should include details of any new, renovated or upgraded **thermal elements**, any new fixed building services, details of their operation and maintenance, any new energy meters and any other details that enable energy consumption to be monitored and controlled.

Data should also be included in the logbook relating to the calculation of the TER and BER. The occupier should also be provided with the recommendations report generated in parallel with the 'on-construction' EPC, which informs the occupier how the energy performance of the building might be further improved.

For guidance and templates, refer to the CIBSE TM 31.[9]

Please refer to Appendix 5.17 for details.

3.3.16 Provide an instruction manual for the fixed building services

The purpose of this is to ensure that the 'owner' and 'occupier' (the terms are used interchangeably in Part L) have all the information needed to run lighting, heating, cooling and ventilation systems effectively and energy efficiently.

An operating and maintenance manual (logbook) is to be provided. CIBSE publication TM 31[9] provides guidance on the content, including standard templates. It is recommended (AD L2A 6.3) that an electronic copy is kept of the energy calculation used for the TER and BER. The TER and BER should be recorded in the logbook.

Designers should ensure that provision of the operating and maintenance manual is included in the contract specification or the mechanical and electrical (M&E) design brief.

Please refer to Appendix 5.18 for details.

Notes

1. *Non-domestic Building Services Compliance Guide.* CLG (2010).
2. *Notice of Approval of the Methodology of Calculation of the Energy Performance of Buildings in England and Wales.* CLG (2008).
3. *National Calculation Methodology (NCM) Modelling Guide (for buildings other than dwellings in England and Wales.* CLG (2010).
4. *Low or Zero Carbon Energy Sources: Strategic Guide.* ODPM (2006).
5. BRE Report BR 262 *Thermal Insulation: Avoiding Risks.* BRE (2001).
6. *Measuring Air Permeability of Building Envelopes.* ATTMA (2006, due to be revised 2010).
7. DW 143 *A Practical Guide to Leakage Testing.* HVCA (2000).
8. CIBSE Code M *Commissioning Management.* CIBSE (2003).
9. CIBSE TM 31 *Building Logbook Toolkit.* CIBSE (2006).

AD L2B: existing buildings other than dwellings

AD L2B *Conservation of Fuel and Power in Existing Buildings other than Dwellings* covers **consequential improvement works** (required when adding an extension or changing a service to a building with a useful area of more than 1000m^2), **extensions to a dwelling** (see note below), **material alterations, material changes of use** or **changes in energy status** of existing buildings as well as replacements of certain services or fittings (called **controlled services** or **controlled fittings**) such as new external doors or windows, new hot water systems, mechanical ventilation and cooling systems, lighting and insulation of existing pipes and ducts, or provision of a new or changed **thermal element** (wall, roof or floor).

4.1 Summary of 2010 changes to AD L2B

The main revisions to AD L2B made in 2010 are summarised below:

1. Energy efficiency requirements now apply to any building space where energy is used to condition the indoor climate (see 4.3 of this guide).
2. **Conservatories** that do not qualify for exemption status need to comply with Part L (see 4.3 of this guide).
3. The definition of **renovation** has been revised.
4. Standards for swimming pool basins in buildings have been defined (see 4.3 of this guide).
5. Guidance on the first fit-out of shell and core developments has been revised.

Please note that extensions of more than 100m² and greater than 25% of the gross area of the existing building are treated as new buildings, and Part L2A should be used (although air permeability testing may not be required if it is impractical; refer to 3.3.12 above).

Enclosing an existing courtyard or enclosing the area under an extending roof is regarded as an extension.

Rooms for residential purposes (nursing homes, student accommodation and so on) are not **dwellings**, and so Part L2B applies to these uses.

4.2 The approaches and requirements vary with the nature of the work

The requirements vary and depend on whether the work is improving a building, providing an extension to an existing building, adding a conservatory, changing the use of the building or making material alterations or whether the work is modifying an existing thermal element or a service. Table 3 shows the requirements for each of the possible approaches.

4.3 Compliance for work to existing buildings other than dwellings

The road map to follow depends on the specific nature of the work to be done, and this is best resolved using either Table 3 or the flow chart (Figure 4). Once it is known which requirements apply, there is a brief explanation in the following text with a more detailed explanation in the appendices.

The broad requirements and the different methods of meeting them are listed in Table 3.

Table 3
Consequential improvements (Section 6 paragraphs 6.1–6.11) – There are three ways to comply: Options 1, 2 or 3

Brief definition	Work that is triggered (as a requirement to the building as a whole) as a consequence of extending an existing building over 1000m² or providing fixed building services or increasing the installed capacity of an existing building service
	The works that trigger the need for consequential improvement works are called the principal works
Option 1 – fabric	Carry out improvements with a simple payback of 15 years such as that described in AD L2B Table 6 (items 1–9) to the extent that their value is not less than 10% of the principal works
	The value is to be demonstrated in a report by a suitably qualified person (e.g. a chartered quantity surveyor)
Option 2 – heating service	If the proposal is for initial provision or increased capacity of a heating service per unit area
	THEN
	Improve the performance of the fabric of the part of the building served by the services (AD L2B 6.10)
	Upgrade those elements below the threshold U-value in Table 5 (paragraphs 5.12 and 5.13)
	AND
	Replace existing doors, windows, roof windows or roof lights with a U-value worse than 3.3W/m²·K (AD L2B 4.23–4.28) (except display windows or high-usage entrance doors)
	AND
	Check that the improvement is technically, functionally and economically feasible (AD L2B 6.5 and 6.6 and section 3.1 – simple payback). Work is required only up to the extent that it complies with Part L (Regulation 17D)
Option 3 – cooling	If the proposal is for the initial provision or increased capacity of a cooling service per unit area
	THEN
	Improve the performance of the fabric of the part of the building served by the services (AD L2B 6.11a)

Table 3
Continued

	Upgrade those elements below the threshold U-value in Table 5(a) (paragraphs 5.9 and 5.10)
	AND
	If the windows (excluding display windows) exceed 40% of the façade area, the roof lights exceed 20% of the roof area and the design solar load exceeds 25W/m²
	THEN (AD L2B 6.11b)
	Upgrade solar controls to achieve:
	a design solar load no greater than 25W/m²
	OR
	a design solar load reduced by 20%
	OR
	an effective g-value no worse than 0.3
	AND
	upgrade the lighting system with an average lamp efficacy of less than 40 lamp-lumens/watt
	AND
	Check that the improvement is technically, functionally and economically feasible (AD L2B 6.5 and 6.6 and Section 3.1). Work is required only up to the extent that it complies with Part L (Regulation 17D)

Extensions (AD L2B 4.3) – may also trigger a consequential improvement

Brief definition	An extension to a dwelling or other building has an element of new-build construction required to enlarge an existing building (enclosing a courtyard or enclosing the area under an extending roof is treated as an extension). A large extension is not treated as work to an existing building if it has an area greater than 100m² and greater than 25% of the existing floor area. In this case, it is regarded as a new building and AD L2A applies (with possible exemption from air permeability testing)

Table 3
Continued

Option 1	Areas of openings comply with Table 2 (AD L2B 4.4)
	AND
	Area-weighted U-values of draughtproofed openings (controlled fittings) to comply with Table 3 (AD L2B 4.3)
	AND
	Fixed building services (such as heating, hot water, pipes, mechanical ventilation, cooling, fixed internal and external lighting – controlled services) comply (AD L2B 4.5, 4.29–4.35)
	AND
	New thermal elements to Table 4 for new elements in an extension (AD L2B 5.1–5.14, 4.3b)
	AND
	As few thermal bridges as possible (AD L2B 5.5–5.7)
	AND
	Reduction of unwanted air leakage (AD L2B 5.5–5.7)
	AND
	Existing opaque fabric that becomes a thermal element (AD L2B 5.12 and 5.13)
Option 2	Show that the CO_2 emission for the actual building plus extension is better than notional building plus extension using an accredited calculation tool (in the calculation, the notional and actual building should incorporate the actual proposed consequential improvements) (paragraph 4.9 and 4.10)
	AND
	Upgrades to existing building no worse than Table 5b (paragraph 4.11)

Conservatories with an area greater than 30m^2 (paragraph 4.13) may also trigger a consequential improvement. Refer to AD L2B (paragraphs 3.21 and 3.22) for a description of when a conservatory is exempt from the energy efficiency requirements

Conservatories	Maintain thermal performance of a wall between a building and a conservatory (paragraph 4.12)
	AND
	U-values of translucent surfaces to comply with Table 4, as for an existing building
	AND
	Any heating service to comply with paragraph 4.12b

Table 3
Continued

Swimming pool basins	Where a swimming pool is provided in a building, the U-value of the basin (walls and floor) should not be worse than 0.25W/m²·K as calculated according to BS EN ISO (British Standards European Norm International Organization for Standardization) 13370 (paragraph 4.14)

Material changes of use or changes in energy status (AD L2B 4.15)

Brief definition	This applies in the case (Part L2B) that a building or a part of a building changes to a use other than as a dwelling (if the change of use is to a dwelling, then AD L1B would apply)
Option 1	U-value of existing openings including roof windows or roof lights less than 3.3W/m² to be replaced (except display windows and high-usage entrance doors) (AD L2B 4.19e) AND Fixed building services (such as heating, hot water, pipes, mechanical ventilation, cooling, fixed internal and external lighting – controlled services) comply (AD L2B 4.20 and 4.23–4.28) AND New thermal elements (AD L2B 4.19b and 5.1–5.7) AND As few thermal bridges as possible (AD L2B 5.5–5.7) AND Reduction of unwanted air leakage (AD L2B 5.5–5.7) AND Renovated thermal elements (AD L2B 4.19, 5.1–5.7). Where any thermal element is being retained, to upgrade it following the guidance given in paragraphs 5.12 and 5.13. This guidance should also be followed in respect of any existing element that becomes part of the thermal envelope of the building where previously it was not (paragraph 4.19d)
Option 2	Calculate whole-building CO_2 emission using an accredited whole-building calculation model to demonstrate that it will become no worse than if following Option 1 (AD L2B 4.21)

Table 3
Continued

Material alterations (AD L2B 4.15)

Brief definition	A material alteration arises when, at any stage, as a consequence of carrying out **building works**, a building or controlled service or controlled fitting no longer complies with the relevant requirements of Part A (structure, changes to fire safety measures under Parts B1, B3, B4 and B5) or under Part M (changes to access and use of buildings)
	(If the building, controlled service or controlled fitting did not comply with these relevant requirements in the first place, a material alteration arises if they become even more unsatisfactory in relation to these requirements)
	When carrying out a material alteration, it will be necessary to comply with the following provisions of Part L2B:
	Existing window and other openings with U-values worse than 3.3W/m^2 to be replaced to comply with AD L2B 4.19c and 4.20–4.23
	AND
	Fixed building services (such as heating, hot water, pipes, mechanical ventilation, cooling, fixed internal and external lighting – controlled services) comply (AD L2B 4.19d and 4.20–4.23)
	AND
	New thermal elements (AD L2B 4.18a and 5.1–5.7)
	AND
	As few thermal bridges as possible (AD L2B 5.1–5.7)
	AND
	Reduction of unwanted air leakage (AD L2B 5.1–5.7)
	AND
	Renovated opaque thermal elements (AD L2B)
	Any element that becomes part of the thermal envelope is to be upgraded to AD L2B 4.19c, 4.20 and 4.23, subject to simple payback calculations

Changes to controlled fittings (AD L2B 4.23–4.28)

Brief definition	Controlled fittings are windows (including the glazed elements of a curtain wall), roof lights and doors (including large access doors for vehicles and roof ventilators) but not display windows or high-usage doors. The term applies to the whole unit, including the frame (AD L2B 4.23)
Reasonable provision	Area-weighted U-value of draughtproof replacement fittings in openings to comply with Table 3 (AD L2B 4.24–4.28)

Table 3
Continued

Changes to controlled services (AD L2B 4.29–4.32) – may also trigger consequential improvement works

Brief definition	Controlled services are heating and hot water systems, pipes and ducts, mechanical ventilation or cooling, fixed internal lighting including display lighting, occupier-controlled external lighting (it does not include emergency or specialist process lighting; refer to note in 4.3.7 of this guide for more details) and renewable energy systems
Reasonable provision	Where work involves the provision or extension of controlled services, **reasonable provision** would be demonstrated by following the guidance set out in the *Non-domestic Building Services Guide*,[1] which includes heating and hot water systems, mechanical ventilation, mechanical cooling air conditioning, fixed internal lighting and renewable energy systems OR For central plant, an efficiency that it is not less than that of the service being replaced (paragraph 41aii)

Changes to a thermal element (AD L2B 5.1–5.14)

Brief definition	A thermal element is a wall (including the opaque elements of a curtain wall), floor, ceiling or roof that separates internal conditioned space from the external environment (Regulation 2A)
New	New thermal elements to comply with Table 4 (AD L2B 5.1–5.4) AND As few thermal bridges as possible (AD L2B 5.5–5.7) AND Reduction of unwanted air leakage (AD L2B 5.5–5.7)
Renovated	Renovation of more than 25%, then thermal elements to comply with Table 5 (AD L2B 5.8–5.10)
Upgraded	Thermal element to be retained that needs to be upgraded in connection with other works (material change of use or when it changes to a thermal element or is part of consequential improvement works) (AD L2B 5.8–5.14) subject to simple payback calculations

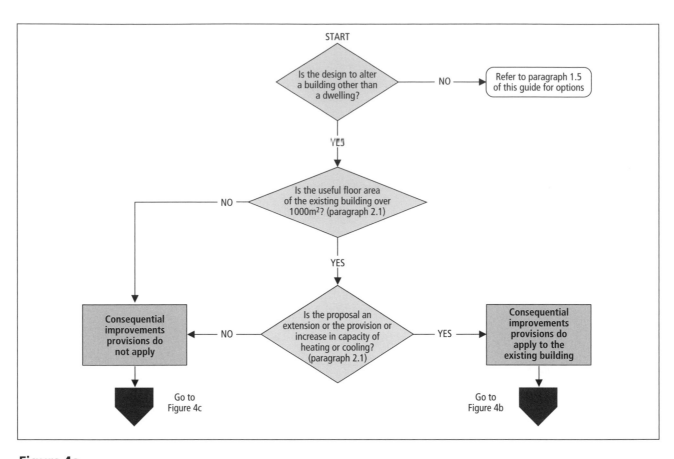

Figure 4a
AD L2B Consequential improvements. Assess the need to provide 'consequential improvements' to the existing building as a result of alterations

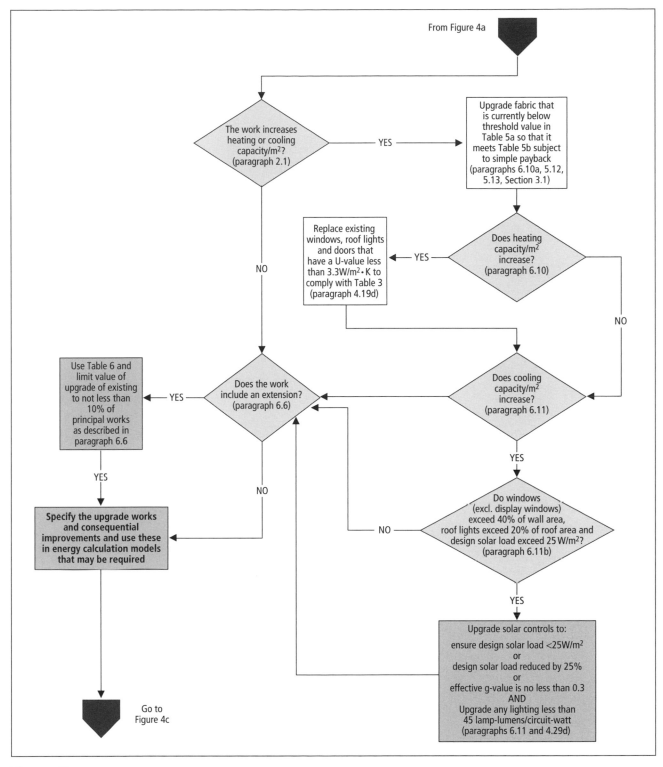

Figure 4b
AD L2B consequential improvements (continued). Assess what 'consequential improvements' are needed to meet the requirements

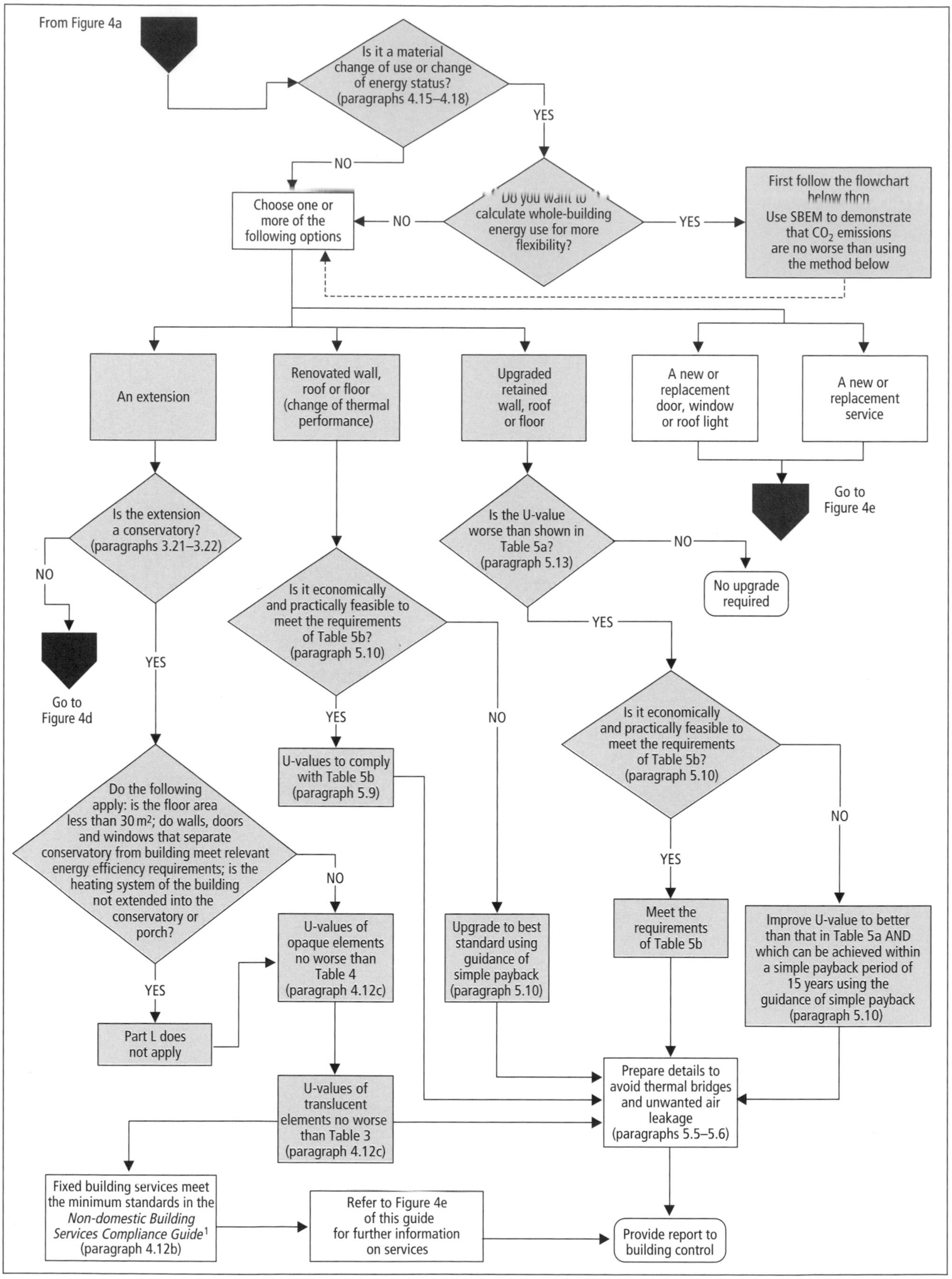

Figure 4c
AD L2B consequential improvements (continued). Walls, roofs, floors and conservatories

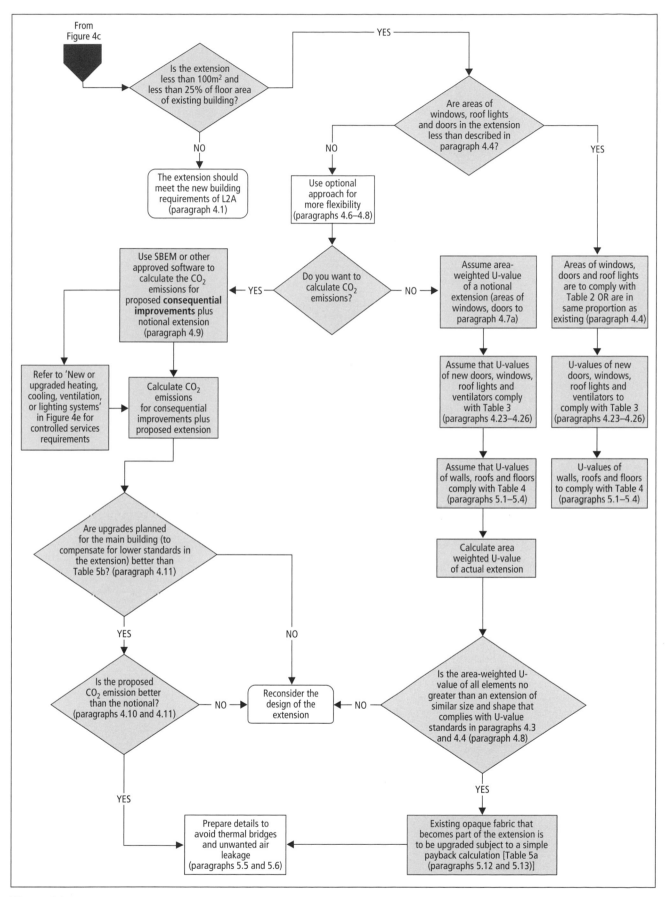

Figure 4d
AD L2B consequential improvements (continued). Designing a new extension

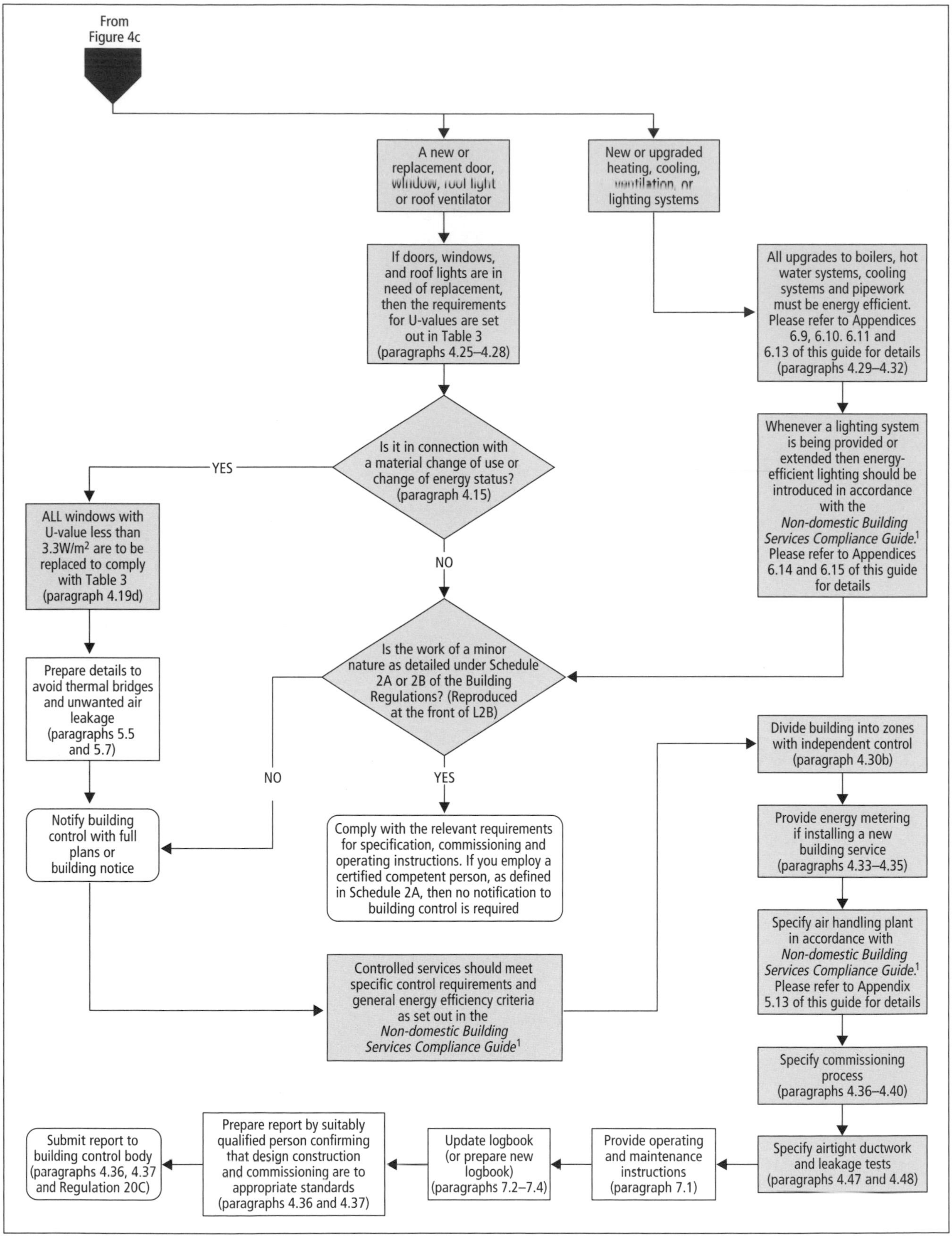

Figure 4e
AD L2B consequential improvements (continued). Windows, doors, roof lights and services

4.3.1 Assess the need to include consequential improvements: Section 6

In principle, this is a simple provision. If certain defined kinds of work are being carried out to a large building with a useful area of over 1000m², then there is a requirement to upgrade the energy conservation performance of that building, provided the upgrade is economically, functionally and technically feasible. These upgrades are called consequential improvements.

The defined kinds of work are building an extension, providing an initial installation of heating and/or cooling and increasing the capacity of heating and/or cooling per square metre. These are called the **principal works**.

The amount that the client will be required to spend on economically feasible consequential improvement works is limited by AD L2B 6.5 to **simple payback** in 15 years and by AD L2B 6.6 to a value not less than 10% of the value of the principal works demonstrated to be the case in a signed report by an **approved competent person** (such as a chartered quantity surveyor).

Table 6 of AD L2B lists some guide measures that would be regarded as economically feasible improvements if the building were being extended. Generally, they focus on upgrading old (more than 15 years old, therefore inefficient) services, introducing energy metering and upgrading the performance of the building thermal envelope. However, there is also the opportunity (if the on-site systems produce less than 10% of the energy demand) to introduce zero- or low-carbon emission energy-generating technology, but the simple payback period has been reduced to seven years for this technology.

If the building work is for an initial installation or an increase in capacity per square metre of heating or cooling, the first priority is to improve the insulation of thermal elements (demonstrating that this is technically and economically feasible using simple payback) and reduce air leakage. The second priority is to upgrade glazed elements, to reduce heat loss in the case of heating or reduce heat gain by solar control shading in the case of cooling. An alternative to providing solar control shading is to provide more efficient lighting systems. There is no 10% limit for these improvements; all cost-effective improvements should be carried out. The 10% limit applies only to extensions.

4.3.2 Justify, if necessary, reduced standards using the 15-year payback criterion

Applies to consequential improvement works or upgrading existing elements owing to a material change of use or where an existing element becomes part of the thermal envelope. It also applies when a window needs to be improved beyond the minimum U-value of 3.3W/m²·K because of consequential improvement works, material changes of use or changes in energy status.

This provision requires that only economically feasible upgrade work, measured using simple payback, needs to be carried out, so permitting some relaxation in the standards of thermal performance required. However, the minimum expenditure required for upgrading elements and fittings is 10% of the cost of the principal works where there are consequential improvements, unless the existing building can be upgraded to a compliant standard for less than this.

4.3.3 Ensure that U-values comply

This section applies to thermal elements (such as new or upgraded walls, roofs and floors) and controlled fittings (such as windows, roof lights, roof windows and doors) in any work to existing buildings.

The designer needs to be able to confirm that the design meets the appropriate criteria at design submission and on completion of construction. If the CO_2 emissions have been calculated using approved energy modelling software, then checks need to be carried out that the specified fittings and elements meet the assumptions of the model. If the window is specified by performance criteria, and thus U-values cannot be calculated, the performance for a standard configuration from BR 443[2] or Table 6e in SAP 2009 can be used. SAP is the government's approved methodology for the energy rating of dwellings, which can be found at http://www.bre.co.uk/sap2009.[3]

AD L2B contains several tables giving U-values for the thermal performance of elements and fittings. For instance, there are a number of different U-value references for walls, floors and glazed elements, so a little care is needed.

Please refer to Appendix 5.6 for details.

Display windows (defined in AD L2B 3.1) do not have to meet U-value standards.

Table 2 in AD L2B shows the area of openings permitted in an extension expressed as a percentage of wall area (or roof area). This can be increased if the percentage of opening in the existing building is already larger than the figures shown in the table.

4.3.4 Show compliance using modelling

Compliance can be shown through modelling either by approved modelling software that follows the NCM or by using SBEM. Please refer to Appendix 5.5 for details of how to show compliance through SBEM.

4.3.5 Confirm that thermal bridges comply and that air leakage is reduced

This section applies in all cases in which thermal performance of an element or fitting has been improved (AD L2B 5.8–5.11).

At the internal surfaces, where insulation is discontinuous or is insufficient (window frames and reveals, at the eaves and so on), the effectiveness of the insulation provided is reduced and cool spots are created where the local inside surface temperature falls below the dew point, causing condensation to form on the inner surface. Guidance can be found on thermal bridging and air permeability in *Limiting Thermal Bridging and Air Leakage: Robust Construction Details for Dwellings and Similar Buildings,* Amendment 1 (TSO, 2002).

BR 262[4] shows how thermal bridging can be avoided by ensuring continuity of insulation at all key junctions. BRE IP 1/06[5] is also referred to in Part L, and this provides guidance on thermal bridges such as those found at junctions of the floor and roof as well as details around window and door openings.

Please refer to Appendix 5.8 for details.

4.3.6 Specify efficient boilers, chillers, pipework, ductwork, fans and controls

The *Non-domestic Building Services Compliance Guide*[1] is a **second-tier document** that sets out clear guidance on means of complying with the requirements of AD L2B with sections on boilers, heat pumps, gas- and oil-fired warm air heaters, gas- and oil-fired radiant technology, CHP, electric space heating, domestic-scale hot water, comfort cooling, air distribution systems, pipework and duct insulation, and renewable energy systems.

The guide sets out the minimum provisions for:

- efficiency of the plant that generates heat, hot water or cooling;
- controls that ensure no unnecessary or excessive use of the systems;
- other factors affecting the safety or energy efficiency of the system;
- insulation of pipes and ducts; and
- acceptable specific fan power ratings for fans serving air distribution systems.

In addition, there is a set of non-prescriptive additional measures to improve plant efficiency.

If the central plant is being replaced, it should meet the requirements of the compliance guide. There are adjustment factors to apply if the fuel source is being changed.

The building should be divided into separately controlled zones (AD L2B 4.30) corresponding to areas with different solar exposures, occupancy periods or activities. The plant for each zone should operate only when required with the default setting as 'off'. The controls required for the type and size of plant are specified in various tables throughout the compliance guide.

Please refer to Appendix 5.10 for details.

Ductwork should be insulated against heat gain/loss (Section 11 and Table 43 of the *Non-domestic Building Services Compliance Guide*)[1] and tested in accordance with the procedures of HVCA DW 143.[6]

Cooling loads should be reduced as much as possible by reducing solar and internal heat gains, and natural ventilation should be used without cooling plant, but only if comfort conditions can be achieved. Fans should meet the requirements of Section 10 and Table 36 of the *Non-domestic Building Services Compliance Guide*.[1]

Pipework should be insulated to Section 11 and Table 41 of the *Non-domestic Building Services Compliance Guide*.[1]

Please refer to Appendices 5.9–5.13 for details.

4.3.7   Provide for energy metering

The requirement under AD L2B is to demonstrate that reasonable provision of energy meters has been made for effective monitoring of the performance of a newly installed plant. The aim is to enable building occupiers to assign at least 90% of their energy consumption of each fuel to the various end uses (such as heating and lighting). Meters should be installed for the services that form part of the works in accordance with the recommendations of CIBSE TM 39. Renewable energy systems should be separately monitored, and, in buildings with a total **useful floor area** of greater than 1000m², automatic meter readings and data collection should be provided (AD L2B 4.33–4.35).

4.3.8   Confirm that lighting is suitably efficient

> Not subject to Part L are emergency escape lighting and specialist process lighting (such as theatre spotlights, projection equipment, TV and photographic studio lighting, medical lighting in operating theatres and doctors' and dentists' surgeries, illuminated signs, coloured or stroboscopic lighting, and art objects with integral lighting such as sculptures, decorative fountains and chandeliers).

Section 12 of the *Non-domestic Building Services Compliance Guide*[1] covers the minimum lighting provision for existing buildings: Table 44 sets out minimum lighting efficacy in existing buildings; Table 45 sets out luminaire control factors for use in existing buildings; and Table 47 sets out controls for general and display lighting in existing buildings.

> Under AD L2B, in existing buildings a control factor can be applied to increase the efficacy of lighting if automatic controls turn off lights when they are not required. This is not an appropriate option in AD L2A, which already takes automatic control into account in the **BER** calculation.

Details of how to calculate this are in Appendix 5.15.

4.3.9   Undertake fabric leakage, ductwork leakage and fan performance testing

> Large extensions that come under the provisions of AD L2A may not require pressure testing owing to the difficulty of containing the extended area. Please refer to Appendix 5.8 for details.

Fabric leakage tests are not required under AD L2B but ductwork should be tested in accordance with the procedures set out in HVCA DW 143[6] on systems served by fans with a design flow rate greater than 1m³/s and on certain classes of high-pressure duct described in HVCA DW 143.[6] The tests should be carried out by a **suitably qualified person** who is a member of the HVCA Specialist Ductwork Group or the Association of Ductwork Contractors and Allied Services (AD L2B 4.47).

4.3.10 Prescribe remedial measures when testing fails

If ductwork fails the leakage tests, carry out remedial work and retesting of new sections as set out in DW 143 *A Practical Guide to Ductwork Leakage Testing*, HVCA, 2000 (AD L2B 4.48).[6]

4.3.11 Prescribe commissioning procedures and certification: logbook

Works to existing buildings require commissioning of all controlled services (heating, hot water, electrical and mechanical) in accordance with CIBSE Code M[7] by a suitable person/organisation, for example a **commissioning specialist** from the Commissioning Specialists Association or the Commissioning Group of the HVCA.

Note also the requirement for ductwork testing described in 4.3.10 above.

Section 7 of AD L2B, paragraphs 7.2–7.4, requires either the update of an existing logbook or the preparation of a new one if one does not exist. The logbook should be suitable for day-to-day use and, if only by summary reference to operating and maintenance manuals or to the CDM *Health and Safety File*, include details of any new, renovated or upgraded thermal elements, any new fixed building services, details of their operation and maintenance, any new energy meters and any other details that enable energy consumption to be monitored and controlled.

For guidance and templates, refer to the CIBSE TM 31 *Building Logbook Toolkit*.[8]

Please refer to Appendix 5.17 for details.

4.3.12 Provide an instruction manual for the heating, cooling, ventilation and lighting systems

The purpose of this is to ensure that the 'owner' and 'occupier' (the terms are used interchangeably in Part L) have all the information needed to run lighting, heating, cooling and ventilation systems effectively and energy efficiently.

An operating and maintenance manual (logbook) is to be provided. CIBSE publication TM 31 provides guidance on the content, including standard templates. It is recommended that an electronic copy be kept of the energy calculation used for **TER** and **DER**. The TER and DER should be recorded in the logbook.

The logbook or equivalent document must be kept up to date with any changes to the building and its systems (AD L2B 7.4).

Designers should ensure that provision of the operating and maintenance manual is included in the contract specification or the M&E design brief.

Please refer to Appendix 5.18 for details.

Notes

1. *Non-domestic Building Services Compliance Guide.* CLG (2010).
2. BR 443 *Conventions for U-value Calculations.* BRE (2006).
3. *The Government's Standard Assessment Procedure for the Energy Rating of Dwellings* (SAP), see http://www.bre.co.uk/sap2009.
4. BRE Report BR 262 *Thermal Insulation: Avoiding Risks.* BRE (2001).
5. BRE Information Paper IP 1/06 *Assessing the Effects of Thermal Bridging at Junctions and Around Openings.* BRE (2006).
6. DW 143 *A Practical Guide to Leakage Testing.* HVCA (2000).
7. CIBSE Code M *Commissioning Management.* CIBSE (2003).
8. CIBSE TM 31 *Building Logbook Toolkit.* CIBSE (2006).

General appendices

5.1 Target emission rate

5.1.1 What is the target emission rate?

The **TER** is the minimum energy performance requirement for new **dwellings**. The TER is expressed as a mass of CO_2 in kilograms per square metre of floor area that should be emitted per year as a result of fixed building services: heating, hot water, ventilation, cooling and internal fixed lighting. The TER for individual dwellings must be calculated using approved software.[1]

5.1.2 Calculate the target emission rate (dwellings)

The TER must be calculated with the same tool as intended for the **DER**.

The builder shall carry out a preliminary calculation before construction begins, based on plans and specifications, and submit these to the BCB as part of the submission of plans. This will produce a list of features of the design that are critical to achieving compliance.

The **TER** is based on the CO_2 emission rates from a notional dwelling of the same size and shape as the actual dwelling and which is constructed according to the reference values set out in Table 4 below. The TER is determined by applying factors for fuel (to reflect implied assumptions about low-carbon energy supplies) and improvement (to reflect implied assumptions about improved fabric and efficiency of building services) to these emissions.

For buildings with more than one dwelling, an average TER for all of the dwellings can be calculated using the following formula:

$$\frac{(TER_1 \times \text{floor area}_1) + (TER_2 \times \text{floor area}_2) + (TER_3 \times \text{floor area}_3)}{(\text{floor area}_1 + \text{floor area}_2 + \text{floor area}_3)}$$

Table 4
SAP guide, Appendix R: reference values (to be used when calculating the CO_2 emissions for a notional dwelling)

Element or system	Value
Size and shape	Same as proposed dwelling
Opening areas (windows and doors)	25% of total floor area (or, if less, the exposed façade area) One opaque door of area 1.85m^2 Any other doors fully glazed
External walls	U = 0.35W/m^2·K
Party walls	U = 0
Floors	U = 0.25W/m^2·K
Roofs	U = 0.16W/m^2·K
Opaque door	U = 2.0W/m^2·K
Windows and glazed door	U = 2.0W/m^2·K Double glazed, low-E hard coat Frame factor 0.7 Solar energy transmittance 0.72 Light transmittance 0.80
Thermal mass	Medium (TMP* = 250 kJ/m²·K)
Living area fraction	Same as proposed dwelling
Shading and orientation	All glazing orientated east/west Average overshading
Number of sheltered sides	Two
Allowance for thermal bridging	0.11 × total exposed surface area (W/K)
Ventilation system	Natural ventilation with intermittent extract fans
Air permeability	10m^3/h·m^2 at 50Pa
Chimneys	None
Open flues	None
Extract fans	Three for dwellings with floor area greater than 80m^2 Two for smaller dwellings
Primary heating fuel (space and water)	Mains gas
Heating system	Boiler and radiators Water pump in heated space
Boiler	Seasonal Efficiency of Domestic Boilers in the UK (SEDBUK 2009) 78% Room sealed Fanned flue On/off burner control
Heating system controls	Programmer, room thermostat and thermostatic radiator valves (TRVs) Boiler interlock

Table 4
Continued

Element or system	Value
Hot water system	Stored hot water, heated by boiler Separate time control for space and water heating
Hot water cylinder	150-l cylinder insulated with 35mm of factory-applied foam
Primary water heating losses	Primary pipework not insulated, cylinder temperature controlled by thermostat
Water use limited to 125l per person per day	No
Secondary space heating	10% electric (panel heaters)
Low-energy light fittings	30% of fixed outlets

*TMP (thermal mass parameter) represents the capacity of building elements to retain heat and/or the potential for overheating.

5.1.3 Calculate the target emission rate (buildings other than dwellings)

The TER for non-dwellings must be calculated with the same tool as the **BER**.

To make these calculations, use SBEM (see Appendix 5.5) or another approved modelling tool.

The TER uses the 2010 notional building (Part L2A paragraph 4.6).

5.1.4 Notional building

The notional building required for the TER calculation:

- is the same size and shape as the proposed building;
- follows the specifications provided in CLG's *NCM Modelling Guide*;[2]
- has the same area of vehicle access doors and display windows as the proposed building;
- excludes any service not covered by Part L, such as emergency lighting, specialist process lighting and lifts (refer to Appendix 5.14 of this guide for the full list of lighting that is not covered by Part L);
- has the same activity areas and class of services as the proposed building using predefined SBEM definitions;
- is subject to occupancy times and environmental conditions in each activity area as defined by the standard data associated with reference schedules; and

- is subject to the climate defined by the CIBSE test reference year for the site as appropriate to location.

Refer to the *NCM Modelling Guide*[2] for seasonal heating system efficiencies and emission factors to be used in the notional building.

The TER is based on a notional building with the amount of glazing as specified in CLG's *NCM Modelling Guide*.[2] Criterion 3 of 2010 Part L is a compliance check for limiting solar gains. Buildings that allow greater solar gain by providing more glazing may have to compensate through enhanced energy efficiency measures in other aspects of the design.

5.2   Calculating the dwelling emission rate

5.2.1   What is the dwelling emission rate?

The DER is the calculated predicted mass of CO_2 emitted by a dwelling per square metre of floor area per year. It is calculated using the SAP (see Appendix 5.4 of this guide) at the preconstruction stage for both the design submission to building control and for the as-built dwelling at practical completion using the results from the air permeability tests. It is a mandatory requirement that the DER must not exceed the TER in order that an EPC can be issued.

5.2.2   Criteria for demonstrating compliance

The need to calculate the DER and show that it is no worse than the TER (see Appendix 5.2.3) is a central requirement of the Building Regulations.

Criterion 1 of AD L1A is achieving an acceptable DER – a predicted rate of CO_2 emissions from the dwelling (the DER) that is not greater than the target rate (the TER). Within this requirement, there is scope to increase or reduce thermal performance of elements, fittings and services, but there are limits on the performance of the building fabric and the fixed building services set by Criterion 2 (see AD L1A 4.18). This is to discourage inappropriate trade-off, for example poor insulation offset by renewable energy systems with uncertain lives. However, to demonstrate the required improvement over the energy performance of a notional building, AD L1A warns that, in order to satisfy the TER, the performance of elements will have to be 'considerably better than the stated values in many aspects of the design' (see note to AD L1A 4.19).

Other factors affecting energy performance are:

- Limiting solar gains in summer – the dwelling must have appropriate passive control measures to limit the effect of solar gains (please refer to Appendix 5.7 for further information). The aim is to reduce or eliminate the need for energy-consuming cooling equipment and to rely on natural ventilation, which will therefore help to improve the DER.
- Quality of construction and commissioning – the quality of construction will be checked throughout the works and on completion to confirm that U-values, thermal bridging, services, controls, lighting and passive solar controls are installed and commissioned as specified in the design DER, and that the building air permeability results are satisfactory in order that an EPC can be issued. If any of these fall short, the option remains to recalculate the DER on the revised values and demonstrate that the DER is still better than the TER.
- Operation and maintenance instructions – 'the necessary provisions for energy-efficient operation'.[3] The incorrect operation and maintenance of boilers, heating, cooling, ventilation and so on will adversely affect thermal performance (Appendix 5.18).

The requirement to meet target carbon emissions applies only to new and not to existing dwellings.

5.2.3 Help with achieving target emission rate and improving dwelling emission rate

The major factors affecting carbon emission calculations are the thermal performance of the thermal envelope, the control of internal and external heat gains, the energy performance of heating and cooling equipment, length and insulation of pipes, efficacy of lighting and the air permeability of the building.

Good overall energy performance can most effectively be achieved through an integrated and holistic approach to design – for example, extra insulation ceases to have real cost-or energy-saving benefits if air leakage is not also reduced.

AD L1A also recognises the following contributions towards improving energy efficiency:

LZC energy supply systems and community energy systems can make substantial contributions to achieving the TER, although the capital costs of some of these solutions may not be economic. Where not installed, buildings can be by made 'LZC ready' so that they can easily be installed at a later date.

Multiple dwellings – a building containing multiple dwellings will achieve compliance if each dwelling has a DER no greater than the corresponding TER or if the average DER is no greater than the average TER (in the latter case, it will still be necessary to provide information for each dwelling).

U-values for elements of the building fabric must be at least as good as those set out in Table 2 of AD L1A.

Design air permeability must be $10m^3/h \cdot m^2$ at 50Pa or better (see AD L1A Table 2). As part of the final DER calculation, air permeability will be based on the results of pressure tests (see Appendix 5.8 of this guide). An assumed air permeability of $15m^3/h \cdot m^2$ will be used for purposes of DER if untested or, where a sample of similar buildings have been tested, the average value of such tests shall be increased by $2m^3/h \cdot m^2$.

Heating and hot water systems must be at least as efficient and meet the minimum control requirements that are recommended in the *Domestic Building Services Compliance Guide*[4] (see Appendices 5.9 and 5.10). Consideration should be given to heating systems that use low distribution temperatures and control systems that give priority to the lowest carbon-intensive sources.

Insulation to pipes, ducts and vessels must be provided to standards not less than those in the *Domestic Building Services Compliance Guide*[4] (Appendix 5.11).

Mechanical ventilation systems must perform no worse than those in *Good Practice Guide* (GPG) 268 (see Appendix 5.12).

Air conditioning must have an energy efficiency rating of greater than 2.4 for air-cooled systems and 2.5 for water-cooled systems. Fixed air conditioners should have an energy efficiency classification equal to or better than class C of the labelling scheme in Schedule 3 of the SI 2005/1726[5] (see Appendix 5.13).

For fixed internal lighting, energy-efficient fittings should be installed in the most frequented areas at not fewer than three per four fixed fittings (see Appendices 5.14 and 5.15).

For fixed external lighting (supplied from the dwelling supply, i.e. not communal), do not exceed 150W per fitting and provide automatic switching when not required (see Appendix 5.14), or compliance for fixed lighting, whether internal or external, would be shown by providing fittings that take only lamps having a luminous efficacy greater than 40 lumens/circuit-watt (see Appendices 5.14 and 5.15).

Fit fluorescent or compact fluorescent light fittings to achieve the above compliances, but not general lighting service (GLS) tungsten or tungsten halogen fittings.

Take appropriate measures to limit solar heat gains in summer, thus reducing or eliminating the need for air conditioning and consequently improving the DER (see Appendix 5.7).

Care must be taken with this area of the design process, as one measure will often have an impact on other areas; for example, smaller windows will mean more use of electric lighting (see BS 8206-2[6] for guidance on adequate levels of daytime lighting).

The TER is based on a notional building with modest amounts of glazing. Buildings that allow greater solar gain will have to compensate through enhanced energy efficiency measures in other aspects of the design (see Appendix 5.7).

Reasonably continuous insulation should be provided over the whole building envelope, avoiding thermal bridges caused by gaps and therefore improving the DER. Refer to BRE IP 1/06[7] and also to BR 262[8] for advice on how to design details and junctions to reduce the risk of thermal bridging.

The process of achieving the target is likely to be iterative. It would be useful to identify those items that can be modified in the software model fairly easily with little cost or design impact on the building itself, for example improve U-values in roofs and walls, try to achieve as much natural ventilation as possible, improve external solar shading design, revise detailing to improve airtightness or provide more efficient heating, cooling or lighting systems.

5.3   Calculating the building emission rate (non-domestic)

5.3.1   What is the building emission rate?

The BER is the weight of CO_2 emitted by the actual building per square metre of floor area. The BER is calculated only for non-domestic buildings, and for dwellings over 450m².

The BER must be calculated with the same NCM-approved tool as the TER. The preliminary calculation is usually carried out as part of the design submission based on plans and specifications, and a final calculation demonstrates that the finished building complies with Part L.

Note that the calculation must be carried out with SBEM (see Appendix 5.5) or other methods as set out in the *Notice of Approval*.[9]

5.3.2 Criteria for demonstrating compliance

Regulation 17C states that 'where a building is erected, it shall not exceed the target CO_2 emission rate'.

The five criteria to demonstrate compliance are:

1. The predicted CO_2 emission rate for the building as constructed (the BER) must not be greater than the TER.
2. The performance of the building fabric and the heating, hot water and fixed lighting systems should achieve reasonable overall standards of energy efficiency.
3. The building has appropriate passive control measures to limit solar gains.
4. The performance of the building as built should be consistent with the prediction made in the BER.
5. The necessary provisions for enabling energy-efficient operation should be put in place.

5.3.3 Help with achieving the target emission rate and improving the building emission rate

The following means can be used to improve energy efficiency:

Grid-displaced electricity, generated by photovoltaic combined heat and power, etc. These emissions will be deducted from total CO_2 emissions before determining the BER.

The use of LZC energy supply systems can make substantial and economically viable contributions towards meeting the TER.[10]

Management features offer improved energy efficiency. Features such as power-factor correction equipment and automatic monitoring with alarms will improve the BER by a significant amount (AD L2A Table 2).

Appropriate controls should be provided to achieve reasonable energy efficiency as follows:

- building subdivision into control zones of differing solar exposure, pattern or use;

- independent timing, temperature control, ventilation and recirculation rates in zones;
- heating and cooling controlled to operate independently; and
- central plant that operates when the zone system requires, for example default is 'off' (see Appendix 5.10).

Appropriate lighting design, controls and management options should be provided, such as avoiding unnecessary lighting of spaces when daylight is sufficient, accessible manual switching, dimmers that reduce rather than divert supply, separate switching of daylit spaces, autoswitching with occupancy or daylight sensors (see Appendices 5.14 and 5.15).

Appropriate energy metering must be provided because 5–10% of the energy being metered can be saved as a result of monitoring energy use.[11]

Reasonable insulation to pipes, ducts and vessels will reduce heat loss, etc., hence improving the BER.

Reasonably continuous insulation should be provided over the whole building envelope, avoiding thermal bridges caused by gaps, therefore improving the BER (see Appendix 5.11).

Carbon emissions associated with a cooling plant can be severe, so careful attention to management of these systems to reduce or eliminate use is a very effective way of reducing the BER.

Appropriate measures to limit solar heat gains in summer, thus reducing or eliminating the need for air conditioning and consequently improving the BER, include size and orientation of the glazed areas, tints, films and coatings in/on the glass, blinds and shading systems such as overhangs, side fins and brise soleils, and using thermal capacity coupled with night ventilation (see Appendix 5.7).

Care must be taken with this area of the design process, as one measure will often have an impact on other areas; for example, smaller windows will mean more use of electric lighting (see BS 8206-2[6] for guidance on adequate levels of day lighting).

The TER is based on a notional building with modest amounts of glazing. Buildings that allow greater solar gain will have to compensate through enhanced energy efficiency measures in other aspects of the design.

As part of the final BER calculation, air permeability/pressure, duct leakage and fan performance tests will be carried out. Guidance on how to achieve a reasonable design air permeability of 10m³/h·m² at 50Pa is given in Appendix 5.8.

Ductwork should be made and assembled so as to be reasonably airtight (see Appendix 5.8).

Note that in buildings of area not greater than 500m², air pressure testing can be avoided if the air permeability figure used in the BER calculation is 15m³/h·m² at 50Pa (improvements to the performance of fabric or services will have to be made in order to meet the TER in this case).

5.4 What is the Standard Assessment Procedure?

5.4.1 What is the Standard Assessment Procedure?

The SAP is the government's approved methodology for rating the energy of dwellings. SAP is now a compulsory component for new dwellings in Part L of the regulations. A SAP assessment is required for all new-build dwellings:

- The procedure for calculating the SAP rating is defined by the published SAP worksheet, which can be downloaded from the SAP website.[1]
- The SAP provides a means of estimating the energy efficiency performance of dwellings. SAP ratings are expressed on a scale of 1–100. The higher the number, the better the rating. It can be likened to 'miles per gallon' when compared with fuel consumption in cars.
- The calculation uses the Building Research Establishment's Domestic Energy Model (BREDEM) to predict heating and hot water costs. The major factors affecting the SAP rating are the insulation and airtightness of the dwelling, and the efficiency and control of the heating and hot water systems.
- SAP programs are used to enter data on the size of the house, its insulation levels, ventilation system and heating/hot water systems.

5.4.2 Information required by the Standard Assessment Procedure

In order to calculate the SAP rating, the model needs the following information on the dwelling and environment. This includes:

- materials used for the construction of the dwelling, including roofs and walls;
- thermal insulation, including the type of thermal insulation materials used in walls, floors or roof construction;
- ventilation characteristics of the dwelling and ventilation equipment, including information on extract fans, opening lights, etc.;
- efficiency and control of the heating system(s);
- efficiency and control of cooling systems (if installed);
- solar gains through openings in the dwelling (orientation can influence solar gain and this information is needed for a SAP calculation);
- the fuel used to provide space and water heating, ventilation and lighting (fuel costs and environmental impact are taken into account when calculating the SAP rating); and
- use of renewable energy technologies.

5.4.3   Output from the Standard Assessment Procedure

The output from the SAP calculation must be certified by an accredited SAP assessor and, for a dwelling, includes:

- DER (kg CO_2/m^2/year): equal to the annual CO_2 emissions per unit floor area for space heating, water heating and ventilation and lighting less the emissions saved by energy generation technologies, expressed in kg/m^2/year;
- fabric energy efficiency;
- energy requirements (kWh/year): the amount of energy required for the heating system;
- fuel costs: fuel prices averaged over the previous three years and across regions; and
- SAP rating: consists of a scale from 1 to 100, where higher is better.

5.4.4   Further information

The 2009 edition of SAP will be introduced from October 2010 and will be used for compliance with Building Regulations in England and Wales (Part L) and in Scotland (Section 6) and for the generation of EPCs for new dwellings.

Further information can be found at the SAP website: http://www.bre.co.uk/sap2009.[1]

5.5   Evaluating energy use and carbon emissions in buildings through the Simplified Building Emission Model

5.5.1   What is the Simplified Building Emission Model?

SBEM is run on an Microsoft Access database and is intended to provide evaluations of energy consumption and carbon emissions in non-domestic buildings as well as domestic buildings over 450m^2.

It was developed by the BRE as part of the NCM for the then Office of the Deputy Prime Minister (ODPM), now the DCLG.[2]

The reports produced by SBEM might assist with the design process, although SBEM is not a design tool and should not be used for making strategic design decisions, and eventually demonstrate whether mandatory carbon emission targets have been met under Part L compliance requirements and for energy performance certification purposes.

The software can be downloaded from http://www.ncm.bre.co.uk/download.jsp together with a user guide for iSBEM, although Microsoft Access 2000 or a later version is required to run it.

The NCM allows the actual calculation to be carried out either by SBEM or by other approved modelling software. It is difficult to give absolute rules about when SBEM can and cannot be used. As broad guidance, it is more likely to be difficult to use SBEM satisfactorily if the building and its systems have features that (a) are not already included in iSBEM and (b) have properties that vary non-linearly over periods of the order of an hour. However, this is not a universal rule. There is a balance between the time and effort required to carry out parametric studies to establish input values for SBEM and detailed explicit modelling of a particular building.

5.5.2   Before using the Simplified Building Emission Model

The inputting screens are not particularly intuitive and take a little getting used to. It is sensible to start by following the tutorial in the iSBEM user guide and/or to attend some formal training on the use of iSBEM (information on organisations that currently offer training on the use of iSBEM can be found at http://www.ncm.bre.co.uk/training.jsp). You may also wish to 'play' with the software before using it in earnest because it is, for example, all too easy to overwrite your records. Playing with the software will also help you to find the gaps where it may be necessary to use default data from the tables in Part L or to carry out some additional research.

First, use Appendix A of the iSBEM user guide to identify the kind of information required in order to use SBEM software. There are useful tips on naming conventions in Chapter 8 of the guide.

Then, before entering the data to calculate the TER for a notional building, it is necessary to use drawings or surveys to identify the various activity zones or the zones that have different lighting, heating or cooling services, or different access to daylight. The spaces in your building will need to be 'zoned' according to the zoning rules specified in CLG's *NCM Modelling Guide*[2] and the guidance provided in the iSBEM user guide. Each of these zones will have a defined geometry and activity that must be set up in the system so that the quantity, construction and orientation of elements, fittings and services can be associated with these zones.

5.5.3   Summary of the Simplified Building Emission Model evaluation process

- Gather the required data for the building.
- Analyse the information and identify the different zones.

Enter the information into the model, double-check your input and run the calculation.

5.5.4   Information required by the Simplified Building Emission Model

In order to calculate energy use and carbon emissions using SBEM, it is necessary to provide information on the following topics.

General information

The first step is to provide general project information including weather (there are 14 available locations for England and Wales, one for Scotland and one for Northern Ireland), building use, ownership and certifier details.

Construction information

The model needs information about the different types of construction used in the building. All of the material information about all types of walls, floors, roofs, doors and glazing in the building is required. This information is then available for selection from a picklist when defining the building geometry.

Geometry and zoning information

> After filling in a field highlighted in green, pressing the 'enter' button allows editing of the entries in the other boxes on the form.

The model contains data on U-values for most standard forms of construction and uses this along with geometry and zoning information to calculate energy losses.

The model uses information about the shape, size and orientation of each zone (activity area) in the building, including the walls, floors, roofs, doors and windows that make up each zone's envelope.

> An activity area is defined as an area that is assigned its own comfort conditions, standard operating pattern and heat gains profile as in the NCM activity database.

Zones need to be defined from analysis of drawings, schedules or survey. The relationship between zones will also have to be considered, along with air permeability, thermal bridging, glazing types and any shading systems used.

Building services information

The model also needs information about all the building systems, including heating and ventilation, hot water, sustainable energy technologies and CHP. Further information on the lighting and ventilation characteristics for each zone is also required, for example:

- heating, ventilation and air conditioning, including system type, fuel, generator efficiency, heat source, cooling system and ventilation, metering, control and adjustments;
- domestic hot water, including fuel, generator type, storage and secondary circulation;

- LZC energy supply systems, including quantity, type, size, inclination and orientation for a solar-powered or photovoltaic system, and quantity, terrain, diameter, hub height and power for a wind-powered system; and
- CHP, including fuel, efficiency and various ratios between space heating, water and so on.

The various building systems must then be assigned to their zones. Information required includes pipe lengths for hot water dead-leg, ventilation type, heat recovery, fan power, lamp type, lighting controls and sensors.

5.5.5 Ratings and outputs generated by the Simplified Building Emission Model

Part L ratings and compliance checking:

- notional BER: CO_2 kg/m² for the notional building;
- TER: CO_2 kg/m²; this is the notional BER;
- BER: CO_2 kg/m² for the actual building;
- pass or fail CO_2 emissions: if the BER is less than the TER, the building passes the CO_2 emissions element of Part L.

Other Part L checks (such as those for U-values) can be found in the documents generated by SBEM.

Asset ratings (and recommendations):

The following information can be provided by SBEM reports:

- the energy used per square metre (kWh/m²) by the actual building and the notional building for heating, cooling, auxiliary energy uses (pumps and fans), lighting and domestic hot water;
- the energy used per square metre (kWh/m²) by the actual building and the notional building in terms of electricity and fuel use;
- the resulting CO_2 emissions (CO_2 kg/m²) from the actual and notional building;
- the percentage of the energy consumed by the notional building that is consumed by the actual building;
- the asset rating (currently the percentage of CO_2 emitted by the actual building out of the total that is virtually emitted by the notional building).

5.5.6   Reports

The Building Regulations compliance document will form part of the submission by designers to building control to demonstrate compliance with AD L2A.

The main output report gives a summary of the energy performance of the building, including:

- details on the building, certifier and building owner;
- whole-building CO_2 performance;
- annual energy consumption by end use; and
- monthly energy consumption by end use.

Data reflection reports contain all the data entered into SBEM for the building and are to be attached to the building logbook.

The technical output report produces data for use in more in-depth analysis of the results, including:

- monthly and annual energy use by fuel type;
- monthly and annual energy use by end use;
- monthly and annual CO_2 emissions; and
- energy production and CO_2 displaced by renewables.

5.6   U-values

5.6.1   What is a U-value?

The U-value (thermal transmittance) of a building element is a measure of the rate of heat flow through the element. Technically, it is calculated as the rate at which heat transfers through $1m^2$ of a structure, with a temperature difference between the internal and external environments of 1°C. The greater the level of insulation of the building element, the lower its U-value, as measured in watts per square metre of area per degree temperature difference across the building element ($W/m^2 \cdot K$). Lower U-values indicate better thermal insulation. For example, a wall with a U-value of 0.3 $W/m^2 \cdot K$ loses heat at half the rate of a wall with a U-value of 0.6 $W/m^2 \cdot K$.

5.6.2   Calculation of U-values

Guidance on the use of calculation methods is contained in BR 443 *Conventions for U-value Calculations*.[12]

There are two ways that U-values can be assessed. Either the individual U-value of an element in a particular plane can be calculated or the average U-value for all elements of the same type can be calculated (the area-weighted average U-value). The area-weighted U-value is used for calculating the heat loss from the building; however, there is a limit on the heat loss allowed for an individual element (the limiting U-value).

There are limits on flexibility for several reasons. There is a risk of creating thermal bridges with the consequent risk of condensation forming internally or within vulnerable parts of the construction. Also, it is not sensible to compensate for poor thermal performance of elements of construction by using highly efficient heating systems of uncertain life.

5.6.3   What is a thermal bridge?

The *Moisture Control Handbook*[13] defines a thermal bridge as a 'region of relatively high heat flow conductance in a building envelope'. An example of a thermal bridge is an uninsulated window lintel or the edge of a concrete floor slab built into a solid blockwork wall. Thermal bridges can have major effects on the thermal performance of building envelopes, significantly increasing winter heat loss and summer heat gain. Further, condensation on thermal bridging elements can result in mould and mildew growth (with accompanying reduction of air quality), staining of surfaces and serious damage to building components.

5.6.4   Assessing cold bridges/thermal bridges

For Building Regulations purposes, one way of demonstrating that a provision has been made to limit thermal bridging at junctions and around openings is to use the details in **ACDs** (see 5.16 of this guide).

As an alternative, accredited experts may calculate the linear thermal transmittance using an established methodology. Where this approach is adopted, the calculated value for linear thermal transmittance should be increased by 0.02W/m·K or 25% (whichever is the greater).

5.6.5   What is condensation?

There are two types of condensation to be concerned about – interstitial condensation and surface condensation. In each case, condensation occurs on cold surfaces when warm, moist air comes into contact with them. This happens when the temperature of the surface is below the so-called 'dew point' temperature of the warm air. As the air in contact with the cold surface is cooled to below its dew point, it must release the excess moisture that it can no longer support. It releases this moisture as liquid water, which appears on the colder surface.

Interstitial condensation

Most building materials, except metals, plastics and similar materials, are to some extent permeable and do not obstruct the movement of moist air through the structure. The warm, moist air can cool to below its dew point within the fabric of the building, resulting in condensation at a layer or air space. Because the condensation is hidden, it can go undetected for long periods, sometimes resulting in serious damage such as timber decay.

Surface condensation

Surface condensation is familiar to most people. It can lead to mould growth, which can be unsightly and can damage decorative finishes. Mould growth can cause a musty odour and can also be a health hazard.

Assessing interstitial condensation risk

To assess the risk of interstitial condensation we need to know two things – the temperature profile through the structure and the vapour resistance of the various layers.

The procedure for assessing the risk of interstitial and surface condensation is described in the British Standard *Code of Practice for Control of Condensation in Buildings.*[14]

Table 5
Summary of all U-values referred to in Part L

	L1A New dwelling		L1B Existing dwelling		
	Table 2 Area-weighted dwelling average	SAP reference value for TER	Table 1 Standards for controlled fittings	Table 4 Standards for new thermal elements	Table 5a Threshold value for upgrading retained thermal elements
Walls (opaque panels curtain walls)	0.3	0.35		0.28	0.7
Cavity wall					0.7
Party wall	0.2		c		
Floor	0.25	0.25		0.22	0.7
Roof	0.2	0.16			
Pitched roof – insulation at ceiling				0.16	0.35
Pitched roof – insulation at rafters				0.18	0.35
Flat roof				0.18	0.35
Window (glazed areas curtain walls)	2.0	2.0[a]	e		
Roof window	2.0		e		
Dormer window side walls					
Roof light	2.2				

Table 3b Improved value for upgrading retained thermal elements	L2A New buildings other than dwellings		L2B Existing buildings other than dwellings			
	Table A1 Cost-effective U-values	Table 4 Limiting U-value standards	Table 3 Standards for controlled fittings	Table 4 Standards for new thermal elements	Table 5a Threshold value for upgrading retained thermal elements	Table 5b Improved value for upgrading thermal elements
0.3	0.3	0.35		0.28		
0.55					0.7	0.55
		g				
0.25		0.25		0.22	0.7	0.25
	0.16	0.25				
0.16	0.16			0.16	0.35	0.16
0.18	0.18			0.18	0.35	0.18
0.18	0.18			0.18	0.35	0.18
		2.2	1.8[b]			
		2.2	1.8[b]			
	0.3					
		2.2	1.8[b]			

Table 5
Continued

	L1A New dwelling		L1B Existing dwelling		
	Table 2 Area-weighted dwelling average	SAP reference value for TER	Table 1 Standards for controlled fittings	Table 4 Standards for new thermal elements	Table 5a Threshold value for upgrading retained thermal elements
Door	2.2	2	1.8		
Glazed door		2.0[a]	1.8		
Vehicle access					
High-use entrances					
Roof ventilation					
Curtain wall					
Display wndows					
Swimming pool basins				0.25	

[a]Double glazed, low-E hard coat, frame factor 0.7, solar energy transmittance 0.72, light transmittance 0.80.

[b]OR window energy rating Band D (in dwelling or building of domestic character) OR centre pane U-value 1.2 $W/m^2 \cdot K$.

[c]OR window energy rating Band E (in dwelling or building of domestic character) OR centre pane U-value 1.2 $W/m^2 \cdot K$.

[d]OR centre pane U-value 1.2 $W/m^2 \cdot K$.

[e]Band C WER (window energy rating).

[f]Cavity party walls to be filled or effectively sealed around the perimeter.

[g]U-value of 0.0 assumed within SBEM for party walls.

Table 3b Improved value for upgrading retained thermal elements	Table A1 Cost-effective U-values	L2A New buildings other than dwellings	L2B Existing buildings other than dwellings				
		Table 4 Limiting U-value standards	Table 3 Standards for controlled fittings	Table 4 Standards for new thermal elements	Table 5a Threshold value for upgrading retained thermal elements	Table 5b Improved value for upgrading thermal elements
		2.2				
			1.8			
		1.5	1.5			
		3.5	3.5			
		3.5	3.5			
		No limit	Exempt			

5.7 Checking for solar gains and overheating

5.7.1 Summer overheating

As insulation levels reduce heat demand, paradoxically, the risk of overheating increases. There are several causes for this. Although solar gain is the primary cause of external heat gain, many causes are internal, for example from cooking and hot water systems, appliances, lighting, computers and people.

Rather than introducing cooling systems that increase energy consumption, the risk of overheating should be limited as far as possible by using passive control measures: appropriate combination of window size and orientation; solar protection through shading and other solar control measures; ventilation (day and night); and high thermal capacity.

Provisions should be made to limit the effect of solar gains on indoor temperatures during summer – this is a requirement for all occupied areas, irrespective of whether or not the building has mechanical cooling (AD L1A 3.27, AD L2A 4.44).

There is no explicit requirement for dealing with summer overheating when carrying out work to an existing building (other than through ventilation for **conservatories**). However, this will be a consideration for dwellings if using modelling calculations (e.g. SAP or SBEM) to demonstrate the improved energy performance in connection with providing an extension or works to create a new dwelling through a **material change of use**. In existing buildings other than dwellings, it may be necessary to consider measures to control solar gain in order to comply with the provisions for **consequential improvement works** resulting from the introduction of a new cooling installation (or if the cooling capacity per unit area of an existing system is being increased).

A means to limit the risk of overheating is to reduce the internal heat gain from lighting (AD L2B 6.11c).

The provisions of Part F will also have to be considered in terms of the contribution to purge and background ventilation.

Designers may wish to go beyond the requirements in the current Building Regulations to consider the impacts of future global warming on the risks of higher internal temperatures occurring more often. CIBSE TM 36[15] gives guidance on this issue.

5.7.2 Reducing the impact of overheating through solar gain

Solar gain is reduced by a combination of choosing an appropriate window size, orientation and shading, and by using high thermal capacity coupled with night ventilation (night air is ventilated into the building to cool, for example, the soffit of an internal concrete floor slab that has a high thermal capacity so that, during the day, the ventilation is closed and the cooled floor slab absorbs heat from the space). External shading (e.g. blinds, awnings, brise soleils, shutters, louvres, balconies over lower storeys or managed vegetation) is much more effective than internal shading at reducing the impact of solar gain, especially when low-E glass is specified. Useful advice can be found in BR 364.[16]

Managed vegetation cannot be relied upon as an effective method of solar shading and may also reduce the amount of daylight below acceptable levels.

Careful orientation of windows at design stage can give benefits in both summer and winter. South-facing glazing can be shaded from high summer sun, but winter sun can pass through the glass and penetrate into the space, increasing solar gain in the winter months and offsetting heating bills. Even without shading there is a benefit because of the differing angles of incidence of the sun's rays on the glass. Large amounts of west-facing glazing should be avoided.

The shading will have a negative influence on available daylight levels.

Window size not only affects solar gain but also impacts on lighting requirements. A small window may reduce thermal gain from outside but, at the same time, the increase in lighting requirement will increase the heat gain from internal lighting systems as well as increasing energy consumption. BS 8206-2[6] contains guidance on providing adequate levels of daylight.

Other factors that influence solar gain are:

• buildings facing due south, which perform better than those facing south-west;[17]
• increasing the thermal mass and increasing the amount that is exposed to the internal environment, which reduces the effect of overheating –

more difficult with lightweight construction such as timber frame or in heavy construction where insulation is applied internally; and

- increasing night ventilation and decreasing day ventilation, which helps keep gains down – the benefit of doing this must be included in instructions to the occupier.

5.8   Designing buildings to control air permeability

5.8.1   What is air permeability?

Air permeability is the uncontrolled leakage of air through the thermal envelope of the building. This uncontrolled and unplanned air flow reduces the effectiveness of the insulated elements, accounts for half the heat loss from building fabric in the UK[18] and adds to the burden on heating and cooling systems (adding up to 40% in energy costs). Controlled air ventilation is necessary, and the requirements are covered in Part F (refer also to *Guide to Part F*).[19]

Part L requires that this uncontrolled air leakage is reduced to an acceptable level and that the results of air permeability tests are taken into account when calculating the energy performance of a building.

Designers will need to ensure that uncontrolled air leakage from the structure will satisfy the air leakage test (subject to the correct quality of workmanship on site being achieved) and so meet the criterion for issue of the EPC.

5.8.2   Causes of air leakage

Air leakage occurs through porous wall constructions, especially mortar joints, the edges of windows, doors, panels, and cladding and around structures or services that penetrate the external envelope of the building.[3] Other routes for air leakage include gaps in curtain walling, at eaves and so on, as well as gaps in windows, under doors, around loft hatches and flush light fittings, poorly fitted ducted extracts, between floorboards and so on. There are also obvious routes for air leakage such as chimney flues.

5.8.3   Design to reduce air leakage

The ultimate responsibility for meeting the requirements of air permeability lies with the constructor. However, the designer will need to provide carefully considered details and performance specifications. Some of the design considerations are as follows:

- Consider the appropriate form of construction for reducing air permeability in the early stages of design.
- Define the heated/cooled zones and, for air leakage purposes, treat them as separate from unheated zones such as service corridors, vertical shafts, boiler rooms and plant rooms.
- Dry forms of construction require particular attention to seal joints between panels, allowing for shrinkage and movement between rigid elements. Flexible joints and seals deteriorate over time, and access should be provided for inspection and replacement to maintain performance. Curtain walling design needs particular attention to the joints between panels and the frame and also where the curtain walling meets other elements, such as the roof and abutting walls. In these cases, a combination of membrane lapped with vertical and horizontal damp-proof membranes together with a mastic seal may be necessary.
- Blockwork is porous and walls that separate zones with different energy performance requirements should be rendered or plastered. Membranes and damp-proof courses should be lapped and sealed.
- All junctions between hard materials (e.g. skirting to floor, wall to plasterboard ceiling) will probably need to be sealed with mastic or gaskets that can be easily replaced. Cavity closing details around windows (including the sill detail) and other thermal envelope penetrations should be carefully sealed to avoid air infiltration. Expanding foam gap filler could be used.
- Seal around holes through concrete floor slabs. Use joist hangers instead of building joist ends in walls.
- Loft hatches can be a significant cause of air leakage.
- Eaves details are a common path for air leakage, and the introduction of a vapour barrier seal here is recommended, taking care not to obstruct the ventilation path to the uninsulated parts of the roof space.
- Gaps in insulation panels in walls are not a cause of air leakage through the thermal envelope, but airflow around the insulation can reduce its effective performance substantially and it would be sensible to specify insulation to have taped tongue and groove joints.

5.8.4 How air leakage testing is undertaken

The approved procedure for pressure testing is the method that tests the building envelope as set out in the **ATTMA** publication *Measuring Air Permeability of Building Envelopes*.[20] The results should be recorded as described in Section 4 of that document.

Testing should be undertaken by either:

- a person registered to test the specific class of building concerned; or
- for dwellings, a person not registered for the class of building concerned, where there is evidence that the test facilities have been calibrated within the previous 12 months using a UK accredited service facility and that the tester has successfully completed a British Institute

of Non-destructive Testing-accredited domestic airtightness training course.

Test results are plotted as flow volume versus pressure difference. The test should be carried out by a **suitably qualified person** (usually a member of the ATTMA), who records design and measured air permeability and confirms in a written report that the approved procedure has been followed. Air permeability should not be less than $10m^3/h \cdot m^2$ at 50Pa, and the BER, when using test results, should be better than the TER.

Air leakage tests are required on virtually all new buildings in order to demonstrate that the designed values have been achieved in the construction phase. The exceptions to this rule are:

- larger housing developments, where sample dwellings can be tested;
- small housing developments (one or two dwellings only), where reference can be made to either:
  - dwellings of a similar type constructed by the same builder and tested in the previous 12 months, or
  - by using a value for air permeability of $15m^3/h \cdot m^2$ at 50Pa when calculating the DER; and
- non-domestic buildings of less than $500m^2$.

If the building is correctly designed (see Appendix 5.8.3), leakage occurs because of failure either to construct the design details correctly or to use the specified detail.

Testing is carried out on the completed building with all 'designed' air paths such as windows, ventilators, chimneys and flues blocked off. Cupboard doors can remain closed; all other internal doors should be wedged open. Drainage traps should contain water. Fire dampers and louvres should be closed, mechanical ventilation systems turned off and the inlet and extract grilles blocked unless the system is being used to provide the air pressure. Lifts and other plant rooms are normally considered to be outside the tested envelope.

The test methodology is based on the premise that the pressure difference is uniform over the entire building envelope.

For domestic buildings, it is normal for the purpose of the test to replace one of the external doors with a blocking piece in which a fan unit is mounted that is capable of producing a pressure difference of 50Pa at a flow rate of $1.0m^3/s$. In order to achieve the same pressure in non-domestic buildings, flow rates of up to $30m^3/s$ will be required and a number of high-volume fans may be used. If the building is mechanically ventilated, it may be possible to use its own heating, ventilation and air-conditioning (HVAC) system to pressurise the building. If this is the case, the outlet vents should be blocked while the inlet vents remain open. Fan capacity should be determined so that a minimum air volume flow rate of 70% of the design rate at 50Pa pressure difference can be maintained.

The test is carried out in stages, with readings being taken at approximately 5-Pa steps (minimum five readings) starting at 10Pa and proceeding up to 55–60Pa. Further readings are taken as the pressure is progressively reduced. If the building is so leaky that the full pressure difference cannot be achieved, extrapolated results can be used provided that a difference of 25Pa can be achieved. Below this level, the results will not be valid.

The effectiveness of any temporary seals should be checked during the course of the test. Failures are usually evident as a result of anomalous readings.

For non-dwellings, ductwork leakage testing should be carried out in accordance with the procedures set out in HVCA DW 143[10] on systems served by fans with a design flow rate greater than 1m^3/s and for those sections of ductwork where:

(a)   the pressure class is such that DW 143[10] recommends testing; or
(b)   for new buildings other than dwellings, the BER calculation assumes a leakage rate for a given section of ductwork that is better than the standard for its particular pressure class. In such cases, any low-pressure ductwork should be tested using the DW 143[10] testing provisions for medium-pressure ductwork. The pressure classes are set out in AD L2A Table 5.

DW 143[10] does not call for any testing of low-pressure ductwork. However, where builders claim that low-pressure ductwork will be less leaky than the normal low-pressure class allowance to achieve an improved BER, this better standard should be demonstrated by testing using the procedures set out for medium-pressure ductwork.

Ductwork leakage testing should be undertaken by a member of the HVCA specialist ductwork group or the Association of Ductwork Contractors and Allied Services.

If a ductwork system fails to meet the leakage standard, remedial work should be carried out and ductwork sections should be retested.

5.8.5   Interpreting the results of an air permeability test

If a test result shows that leakage is higher than anticipated, it is recommended that suspect details are selectively blanked off temporarily and the test re-run. This should give valuable information with regard to the design of remedial measures.

Test results are plotted as flow volume versus pressure difference; the requirement is that both the upward and downward curves appear to be reasonably smooth. If this is the case, the 50Pa value (or extrapolated value) represents the test result and should be divided by the area (m²) of the building envelope being tested (including the ground floor) to give the air permeability in m³/h·m² of the building envelope.

If a building fails to achieve its design air permeability, it may still meet the requirements if it achieves both the target air permeability and DER (or BER for buildings other than dwellings). A construction failing on both of these criteria must be retested following the implementation of remedial measures.

5.9   What is an efficient boiler?

The *Domestic Building Services Compliance Guide*[4] sets out clear guidance on means of complying with the requirements of Parts L1A and L1B with sections on gas- and oil-fired heating, hot water systems, electric, solid fuel, community, underfloor and heat pump heating systems (with further sections on solar heating, CHP and other LZC energy systems, ventilation and comfort cooling). Once the method of providing hot water and heating has been decided, then the tables in each section provide the target performance and criteria for the boiler, cylinder, pipe work, radiators and controls.

The *Non-domestic Building Services Compliance Guide*[21] sets out clear guidance on means of complying with the requirements of Part L2A and Part L2B, with sections on boilers, heat pumps, gas- and oil-fired warm air heaters, gas- and oil-fired radiant technology, CHP, electric space heating, domestic hot water, comfort cooling, air distribution systems, pipework and duct insulation, wind-powered electricity-generating systems, solar photovoltaic systems, lighting, heating system glandless circulators and water pumps. The guide also includes a compliance checklist and a tool for data input into the NCM.

Boiler efficiency is not a constant, and varies according to the season of the year and the varying loads placed on the boiler. For gas and oil boilers, the appropriate seasonal efficiency is determined from a standard test appropriate to the UK, known as the SEDBUK method. All new gas and oil boilers are rated by an independently certified test and placed on the boiler efficiency database at http://www.sedbuk.com. The list is updated monthly.

The efficiency of new boilers varies between about 70% and 90%. Condensing boilers (gas and oil) are more efficient but may be more expensive to purchase. The *Domestic Building Services Compliance Guide*[4] states that, for new or replacement gas-fired boilers, 'the boiler efficiency should not be less than 90% (SEDBUK)'.

Table 6
What is an efficient boiler? Typical comparison factors with a new condensing boiler (value 1.0) for different property types, based on the annual fuel cost estimator at http://www.sedbuk.com/

Boiler type	Seasonal efficiency	Flat	Bungalow	Terraced	Semi-detached	Detached
Old heavyweight	55%	1.50	1.52	1.52	1.53	1.55
Old lightweight	65%	1.30	1.31	1.31	1.31	1.33
New non-condensing	78%	1.08	1.11	1.11	1.11	1.12
New condensing	88%	1.00	1.00	1.00	1.00	1.00

It therefore costs 33% more to operate an old lightweight boiler in a typical detached house than a new condensing boiler.

Default efficiency values for all types of boilers are published in Table 4 of the SAP rating guide, which can be found at http://www.bre.co.uk/sap2009.[1]

The preferred order for establishing the seasonal efficiency for a boiler is:

1. Consult the boiler efficiency database.
2. For new gas- and oil-fired boilers not listed in the boiler database, obtain a declaration of the SAP value from the manufacturer, if available.
3. If information is not available using methods 1 and 2, and for all other fuel sources, use Table 4a or Table 4b in the SAP specification.
4. Add efficiency adjustments from Table 4c in the SAP specification.

If equipment is being replaced, in non-domestic buildings there is scope to 'earn' heating efficiency credits to improve its effective heat-generating seasonal efficiency rating for incorporation into SBEM or another accredited modelling tool. A list of credit scores is included in Table 8 of the *Non-domestic Building Services Compliance Guide*[21] and they are awarded for reducing overdesign of boilers, introduction of weather compensation valves, optimised start/stop control systems, full building management systems and other such options.

There is a compliance checklist in Appendix 2 of the *Non-domestic Heating, Cooling and Ventilation Compliance Guide*.

5.10 What are efficient heating controls?

5.10.1 Buildings other than dwellings

The *Non-domestic Building Services Compliance Guide*[21] refers to the 'minimum controls package', which represents the minimum requirement for each technology necessary to comply with AD L2A and AD L2B.

The requirements for the minimum controls package are different for each type of system.

For example, Table 5 in the *Non-domestic Building Services Compliance Guide*[21] describes three packages, each applying to a different boiler plant output. As the output of the boiler increases, the controls requirement increases. A boiler of less than 100kW needs timing and temperature controls (in zones where the building area is greater than 150m^2) and weather compensation (except where constant temperature supply is required). However, a larger boiler of less than 500kW also needs optimal start/stop controls with night set-back (or frost protection outside occupied periods) and two-stage high-/low-firing facility (or multiple boilers with sequence controllers). Individual boilers larger than 500kW require fully modular burner controls rather than two-stage firing.

5.10.2 Dwellings

The *Domestic Building Services Compliance Guide*[4] sets out the minimum requirements of AD L1A and AD L1B for controls for each of the systems covered by the guide. The requirements are different for each type of system.

For example, Table 2 in the *Domestic Building Services Compliance Guide*[4] describes the controls that are required for a gas-fired wet heating system: boiler interlock (so that boilers and pumps do not operate when there is no demand for heat); time and temperature control of space heating; separate zoning for heating and hot water, each of which must serve an area of no more than 150m^2; separate time control of hot water (other than where provided by instantaneous heaters); and temperature control of hot water. For gas-fired wet heating systems, the provisions for replacement systems are the same as for new installations.

The various systems covered by the *Domestic Building Services Compliance Guide*[4] come under the following groups:

1. boilers with wet heating systems (radiators or underfloor heating);
2. electric heating systems;
3. solid fuel heating systems;
4. ventilation/warm air systems;
5. heat pumps;
6. community heating schemes (seek specialist advice);
7. room heaters; and
8. other systems.

Within SAP, the efficiency of the primary heating source can be further enhanced (or degraded) by the level of control available, having a positive (or negative effect) on the DER. The SAP specification identifies various types of control applicable to different types of heating system, which, if used either singly or in combination, can improve performance. These are as follows:

Room thermostat

Switches space heating on/off at a single adjustable temperature that is preset by the user.

Time switch

Controls either space heating or hot water for one or more on/off cycles per day, repeated over a daily or weekly cycle.

Programmer

Time switch capable of controlling space heating and hot water independently.

Programmable room thermostat

Combined room thermostat and time switch.

Delayed-start thermostat

Delays timed heating dependent on internal or external temperature.

Thermostatic radiator valve

Controls heat output of a radiator according to air temperature.

Cylinder thermostat

Switches water heating on/off at a single user-adjustable temperature.

Flow switch

Switches system off, for example when all TRVs are closed.

Boiler interlock

Controls arrangement preventing boiler firing when there is no heat demand.

Bypass

Arrangement of pipes to ensure that minimum flow rate is maintained in the boiler.

Boiler energy manager

Varies in complexity from a simple device to delay boiler firing to full optimisation control.

Time and temperature zone controls

Minimum two zones with independent time and temperature controls.

Weather compensator

Senses and limits system water temperature according to external temperature.

Load compensator

Senses and limits system water temperature according to internal temperature.

Controls for electric storage heaters

- manual charge control – adjusted by user;
- automatic charge control – using internal or external temperature sensors; and
- CELECT-type controller – electronic control of heaters.

5.11 How to insulate pipes, ducts, tanks and cylinders

5.11.1 General

Pipes, ducts and equipment require insulation to protect against heat loss; to keep temperatures constant; minimise the risk of damage by frost or freezing, condensation or fire; and to provide an element of acoustic protection and safety in keeping human contact with very hot or cold surfaces to a minimum.[22]

The type of insulation will depend on the range of operating temperatures for the circuit and the location of the equipment, for example whether it is internal or external or above or below ground.

For small- to medium-bore pipes (domestic or small commercial installations), a one-piece preformed insulation is usually appropriate. Examples of this may be wool, felt, cork, flexible rubber or fibreglass. Larger bore pipes over 250mm diameter will require a quilted material secured with metal bands or adhesive tape with taped joints.

Rectangular ducts and tanks should have a rigid or semi-rigid slab insulation, cut to fit with overlaps at angles and bonded as recommended by the manufacturer. Duct insulation should be covered with an impermeable finish to provide protection and shed condensation. In external situations, this should be a sheet metal protection for additional strength.

Cylinders can be insulated using the same method as tanks, although both tanks and cylinders in domestic situations can be fitted with a quilted jacket. New domestic cylinders are usually insulated with foam before they are installed.

5.11.2 Dwellings

Tables 3, 11, 16, 22 and 28 of the *Domestic Building Services Compliance Guide*[4] describe the minimum provision for the insulation of pipes serving new and replacement gas, oil, electric boiler, solid fuel-fired and community central heating systems.

Primary circulation pipes should be insulated whenever they pass outside the heated living space, domestic hot water pipes should be insulated throughout their length (except where impractical – for example, through joists) and all pipes connected to hot water storage vessels should be insulated for 1m from their point of connection to the cylinder (or to where they become concealed). Lesser standards are acceptable for replacement systems where access is unavailable. Buried community heating pipes tend to be pre-insulated to BS EN 253,[23] but variable volume controls assist by maintaining low return temperatures (and correspondingly lower rates of heat loss).

Table 39 of the *Domestic Heating Compliance Guide* requires that all primary circuit pipes should be insulated for solar hot water systems throughout their length. Pipes connected to hot water storage vessels are as described in the preceding paragraph.

All insulation should be labelled as complying with the *Domestic Building Services Compliance Guide*[4] (or lesser standard where there are constraints).

5.11.3 Buildings other than dwellings

Pipes and ducts are insulated to avoid heat loss in heating systems and heat gain in cooling systems.

The *Non-domestic Building Services Compliance Guide*[21] covers pipework and ductwork insulation. It requires that all hot water and heating pipework be insulated so that heat loss occurs only where 'it is useful'. Maximum heat loss requirements to determine required insulation levels are given in Table 41 of the compliance guide.

The cooling load to compensate for heat gain in distribution pipework should be less than 5% of the total load. Maximum heat gain requirements to determine required insulation levels are given in Table 42 of the compliance guide.

Where the same ducting is used for heating and cooling, it should meet the requirements for chilled ductwork in accordance with Table 43 in the compliance guide – heat loss/gain per unit area, heat gains being expressed as a negative value.

5.12 How to provide an acceptable ventilation system

5.12.1 General

The most energy-efficient solutions will be achieved in buildings with low air permeability that have properly designed (natural or mechanical) ventilation. The companion *Guide to Part F*[19] describes minimum ventilation requirements. In some circumstances, a mechanical system will be required to control external noise or pollutants.

Minimising internal and external heat gains is a key part of an energy-efficient ventilation strategy.

Please refer to Appendix 5.8 for further information.

5.12.2 Dwellings

Guide to Part F[19] the companion guide to this document, sets out the requirements for the following ventilation systems in dwellings:

- background ventilators and intermittent extract fans;
- passive stack ventilation;
- continuous mechanical extract; and
- continuous mechanical supply and extract with heat recovery (MVHR).

Where mechanical ventilation systems are installed in dwellings, these should:

- follow the guidance in GBG 268[24] and the CLG publication *Domestic Ventilation Compliance Guide;*[25] and
- meet the minimum standards set out in Table 32 of the *Domestic Building Services Compliance Guide,*[4] reproduced below.

Table 7
Minimum provisions for mechanical ventilations systems

	Standards for new and replacement systems	Supplementary information
Fan power	Mechanical ventilation systems should be designed to minimise electric fan power. Specific fan power (SFP) should not be worse than: 0.5W/l/s for intermittent extract ventilation systems; 0.7W/l/s for continuous extract ventilation systems; 0.5W/l/s for continuous supply ventilation systems; 1.5W/l/s for continuous supply and extract with heat recovery ventilation systems	
Heat recovery efficiency	The heat recovery efficiency of balanced mechanical ventilation systems incorporating heat recovery should not be worse than 70%	
Controls	Intermittent mechanical extract ventilation systems should be operated by local manual switches or automatically by a presence sensor. All other mechanical ventilation systems should have manual or automatic control of the boost facility	BS EN 15232:2007 *Energy Performance of Buildings – Impact of Building Automation, Controls and Building Management*

5.12.3 Buildings other than dwellings

Details can be found in Section 10, Air Distribution Systems, in the *Non-domestic Building Services Compliance Guide*,[21] which describes the requirements for both central and local ventilation systems (with and without heating, cooling and heat recovery).

Table 36 of the compliance guide shows limiting specific fan powers in W/l/s for various system types for new buildings. The values for existing buildings are shown in Table 39 of the compliance guide. Fan power is a factor of energy modelling calculations; in SBEM, there is an option to use the default, which is set at 3W/l/s.

Ductwork should have minimal leakage. A way of achieving this is to fabricate the ducts to the specifications given in HVCA DW 144[26] The SBEM gives better results for calculations if leak tests for ductwork and air-handling units meet the CEN [Comité Européen de Normalisation (The European Committee for Standardisation)] classifications. There is specific guidance on ventilation for hospitals and schools published by NHS[27] and DCSF,[28] respectively.

Part L requires that ventilation systems have effective controls, appropriate commissioning and the provision of operating systems and instructions. Information on appropriate controls for different sizes of plant is set out in Table 38 of the *Non-domestic Building Services Compliance Guide.*[21]

5.13 What is an efficient air-conditioning system?

5.13.1 Dwellings

Fixed air-conditioning units for use in dwellings are required to be labelled with an energy efficiency classification graded from classes A to G.[23] Class A represents the most energy efficient and G the least.

For room air conditioners, the efficiency is indicated by the energy efficiency ratio (EER), which is the ratio of cooling to power consumption. The higher the EER rating, the more efficient the air conditioner.

The minimum standards for air conditioners are set out in the *Domestic Building Services Compliance Guide.*[4] Table 36 sets out the following minimum standards for new and replacement systems:

- air-cooled air conditioners: EER greater than 2.4 when operating in cooling mode;
- water-cooled air conditioners: EER greater than 2.4 when operating in cooling mode;
- fixed air conditioners: energy efficiency classification equal to or better than class C.

The installation should be carried out by a competent refrigeration and air-conditioning engineer with a valid refrigerant-handling certificate and the installer should be approved by the manufacturer or supplier of the equipment.

Pipes as well as ducts carrying treated air should be insulated and enclosed in protective trunking to limit accidental damage.

It will also be necessary to consider the impact of internal and external thermal heat gains (see Appendix 5.7) and to meet the requirements for ventilation under Part F.

5.13.2 Buildings other than dwellings

The initial emphasis is on reducing internal and external heat gains to minimise the requirement for air conditioning. See Appendix 5.7 for guidance on solar control strategies, reducing heat gains to cooling equipment, reducing air leakage from buildings and ductwork and providing suitable controls, appropriate commissioning and operating systems/instructions to enable energy-efficient operation of the building.

Section 9 of the *Non-domestic Building Services Compliance Guide*[21] covers comfort cooling. The guide explains the significance of the seasonal energy efficiency ratio (SEER), which is dependant on system performance at various levels of part-load. It also covers the minimum provisions for comfort cooling in new and existing buildings. Values for the minimum EER for comfort cooling are given in Table 34. Table 35 covers minimum controls for comfort cooling in new and existing buildings

5.13.3 System design

Each zone (defined by activity, internal or external thermal gains or independent conditioning systems) should be considered independently.

The designer may have to consider the long-term use of the building and its ability to be readily adapted to meet the changing needs of the user. This will determine the requirement for in-built flexibility of air-conditioning systems.

The SBEM calculator includes various choices for air-conditioning systems, each of which has default values for the CO_2 emissions for a variety of fuel sources. The emission factors for a variety of fuel sources are given in Table 2 of the *NCM Modelling Guide*.[2]

Improvements can be made in energy performance by using one or more of the following approaches:

- Consider the use of heat recovery systems.
- The system itself should not be overdesigned and should be optimised for each zone.
- The design should take into account ease of access for repairs and replacements of the plant and the controls.
- Efficiency is optimised by the use of variable speed-driven primary and secondary pumps.
- Paragraph AD L2B 4.34 requires the provision of energy metering on newly installed plant.
- Primary pipes containing conditioned fluid should be as short as possible and well insulated to avoid heat gain of coolant.
- Pipework and ductwork needs to be insulated to standards set out in Section 11 of the *Non-domestic Building Services Compliance Guide*.[21]
- Consider increasing temperatures and differential temperatures (to reduce unwanted heat gain) and reducing flow rates (this reduces the energy used by pumps).
- Consider improving airflow in (less resistance) ductwork (to reduce fan energy).

Enhanced capital allowances (ECAs) enable businesses to claim 100% first-year capital allowances on their spending on qualifying plant and machinery. Businesses can write off the whole of the capital cost of their investment in certain energy-conserving technologies against their taxable profits for the period during which they make the investment. Details can be found on http://www.eca.gov.uk.

Controls

The *Non-domestic Building Services Compliance Guide*[21] requires that individual cooling modules are provided with controls that provide the most efficient operation of combined plants, and that the cooling systems are capable of time and temperature control at each terminal (through either integral or remote controls) and prevent simultaneous heating and cooling at each terminal:

- The system controls should be readily accessible so that they run the plant only when it is required and can be easily overridden if necessary.
- Consider the use of refrigerant loss monitors; note that an annual check will be required when there is more than 3kg of refrigerant in the system.
- Table 2 of Part L2A gives beneficial adjustment factors for CO_2 emissions if automatic monitoring systems with alarms are incorporated into the design.

Commissioning

- Ductwork on systems served by fans with a design flow rate greater than 1m³/s (and also ducts designed for the BER to have leak rates lower than the standard) should be tested for leakage (paragraph 5.19b of Part L2A) in accordance with procedures set out in HVCA DW 143[10] and by an **approved competent person** (e.g. a member of the HVCA Specialist Ductwork Group or a member of the Association of Ductwork Contractors and Allied Services).
- A logbook should be provided in accordance with paragraph 6.2 of Part L2A (a way of showing compliance is using CIBSE TM 31[29] *Building Logbook Toolkit*). The logbook must include the information used to calculate the TER and BER.
- For existing buildings under Part L2B, a new or updated logbook should be provided that should include details of newly provided services, their operation and maintenance, and any newly installed energy meters (see Appendix 5.18).

Operation and maintenance

Instructions should include:

- regular calibration of controls;
- regular cleaning of dirty filters and clearing dust from fins; and
- regular inspection of ductwork to ensure that insulation and airtightness are maintained.

These checks aim to avoid too much deterioration in the energy performance of the system.

5.14 What are energy-efficient light fittings?

Replacing old lighting with modern fittings that include high-frequency electronic ballasts, high-efficiency tubes and high-efficacy reflectors can significantly reduce energy consumption.

Lighting ballasts is the generic term for electrical or electronic components that are required to control the current passing through fluorescent discharge tubes. These ballasts dissipate energy and can affect the light output efficiency of the tube itself.

These measures are particularly relevant to non-domestic installations, although low-output fluorescent lamps can be used successfully in domestic situations, with the lamps lasting up to 12 times longer than the equivalent standard incandescent lamp.

Low-energy lamps, such as compact fluorescents, generally have an average light output equivalent to five times their power consumption, for example a low-energy lamp consuming 15W of power will have a light output in the region of 75W.

All four sections of Part L require fittings to be installed that can accept only low-energy lamps. Details of the requirements have been included in Chapters 2, 3, 4 and 5 of this guide, and are reproduced below:

Dwellings – internal lighting

• No fewer than three of four of all the light fittings in the main dwelling spaces should be low-energy fittings.

• Low-energy light fittings should have lamps with a luminous efficacy greater than 45 lamp-lumens/circuit-watt and a total output greater than 400 lamp-lumens (excludes light fittings whose supplied power is less than 5 circuit-watts).

Dwellings – external lighting

Either:

• lamp capacity not greater than 100 lamp-watts per fitting and automatically controlled by daylight sensors and occupancy detection;

or:

• where manually operated, lamp efficacy to be greater than 45 lumens/ circuit-watt and automatically controlled by daylight sensors.

Non-dwellings – general lighting

• Average initial efficacy should be not less than 55 luminaire-lumens /circuit-watt [control factors in Table 8 (below) apply to existing buildings for office, industrial and storage areas].

Non-dwellings – display lighting

• Average initial efficacy should be not less than 22 lamp-lumens/circuit-watt.

Reasonable provision is to locate lighting controls where they would encourage occupiers to switch off lighting when there is sufficient daylight or the space is not in use. Local controls should be no more than 6m away from the luminaire (or a distance of twice the luminaire height from the floor if this is greater). Dimming should be by reduction (and not diversion) of the power supply.

5.15 How to calculate luminaire-lumens/ circuit-watt

This calculation will not normally be required in order to comply with Parts L1A and L1B. For most domestic situations, it will generally be adequate to provide fittings that accept only energy-efficient light bulbs (see 1.3.6 and 2.2.8 of this guide). This will have the effect of limiting the luminaire efficacy (nlum) to 40 luminaire-lumens/circuit-watt. For Parts L2A and L2B, the calculation below may be used to calculate the value of nlum.

> Two units have been used – 'luminaire-lumens/circuit-watt' and 'lamp-lumens/circuit-watt'. A luminaire contains one or more lamps housed in a fitting, and care must be taken to ensure that the correct units are being applied.

A step-by-step guide follows.

For each luminaire:

1. Establish the average initial (100h) lumen output (phi lamp) for each lamp in the luminaire and add them together (A).
2. Multiply A by the light output ratio (LOR)* of the luminaire to give B.
3. Divide B by the luminaire control factor (C_L) taken from the table to give C.

For the building:

1. Sum the values of C for each luminaire and divide by the sum of the circuit-watts (P) for all the luminaires to give the luminaire efficacy (nlum).

*LOR is defined as the ratio of the total light output of a luminaire under stated practical conditions to that of the lamp or lamps under reference conditions.

Table 8
Luminaire control factors used to calculate luminaire-lumens/circuit-watt

Control function		C_L
(A)	Luminaire in daylit space with photoelectric switching or dimming with or without local manual override	0.90
(B)	Luminaire in generally unoccupied space with manual on-switching but sensor-controlled off-switching where absence is detected	0.90
(C)	Both (A) and (B) above are provided	0.85
(D)	In all other circumstances	1.00

C_L, value of luminaire control factor.

5.16 Accredited construction details and model designs

ACDs have been introduced to assist the construction industry with achieving the performance standards required to demonstrate compliance with the energy efficiency requirements of Part L of the Building Regulations.

As U-values are progressively tightened, air leakage and thermal bridging become an increasingly significant part of envelope heat loss. Consequently, it is important that careful attention is given to junction details so that the continuity of both the insulation layer and the air barrier is maintained, consideration is given to the buildability of details and evidence is available to show that the intended performance levels have been achieved in practice.

In 2006, CLG published a series of generic ACDs that assist building designers and developers to comply with the thermal and airtightness performance standards published in the 2006 AD L, and the Energy Saving Trust (EST) has published a portfolio of 'enhanced' construction details.[24] These details cover standardised domestic-style construction and are therefore limited in their application. There is increasing crossover between the methods of construction adopted for the domestic and non-domestic sectors, and there is logic in developing this scheme to cover both dwellings and non-domestic construction.

CLG is proposing that a more comprehensive approach to ACDs is developed through an industry-led scheme that achieves the performance levels set out in BRE IP 1/06[7] following established modelling methods based on BR 497,[30] enhances confidence in the buildability of the details and includes inspection to gain feedback.

CLG will consider how to set criteria for the scheme so that:

- Predicted performance is calculated by suitably qualified and experienced individuals using appropriate calculation tools and methods.
- An assessment panel of suitably qualified and experienced assessors can provide confirmation of the buildability and practicality of a detail.
- Inspection systems gather necessary data and evidence gathered is fed back into the assessment of the published details.
- The thermal bridge allowance appropriate to the package of selected details is fed appropriately into the CO_2 emission rate calculation.

Areas for consideration during assessment are:

1. air barrier continuity;
2. thermal insulation; and
3. vapour control.

Individual products or system types will raise specific issues in relation to these three aspects of performance, and it will fall on the assessors to identify these and review the details accordingly.

Standardised sheets are anticipated for each detail to include, but not be limited to, the following:

- 1:10 detail drawing in either 2D or 3D;
- component product specifications and references;
- calculated performance values and factors together with approved modeller details;
- identification of airtight barrier (position and composition) and insulation;
- continuity;
- vapour control layers; and
- guidance on the specific construction sequence and required skills to help site staff to assemble the detail in the best way.

An essential element of the scheme is the inspection regime that monitors the implementation of the accredited details on site, thereby giving added confidence that the claimed performance levels are being realised in practice. A further benefit of the inspection regime would be to get field evidence of the practical buildability of the details.

Some builders may prefer to adopt model design packages rather than to engage in design for themselves. These model packages of fabric U-values, boiler seasonal efficiencies, window opening allowances, etc. should achieve compliant overall performance within certain constraints. The construction industry may develop model designs for this purpose, with information about such designs being made available at http://www.modeldesigns.info.

It will still be necessary to demonstrate compliance in the particular case by showing that the DER or BER is no worse than the TER.

5.17 How is a system properly commissioned?

5.17.1 Dwellings

Commissioning includes setting to work, regulation (that is testing and adjusting repetitively) to achieve the specified performance, the calibration, setting up and testing of the associated automatic control systems, and recording of the system settings and the performance test results that have been accepted as satisfactory.

Reasonable provision would be to ensure that every system has been inspected in an appropriate sequence and to a reasonable standard in accordance with a commissioning plan, and that the test results are reasonably consistent with the design requirements. The commissioning plan should be submitted with other plans submitted to the BCB so that it can check that the commissioning is being undertaken as specified as the work proceeds.

The provisions are identical for the construction of a new dwelling, **extension to a dwelling**, installation of a new system and modification to existing systems.

The heating, hot water and ventilation system(s) should be commissioned so that, at completion, the system(s) and their controls are left in working order and can operate efficiently for the purpose of the conservation of fuel and power.

Advice is available within the *Domestic Building Services Compliance Guide*[4] for heating and hot water systems and within the *Domestic Ventilation Compliance Guide*[25] for ventilation systems.

> An approved competent person must certify commissioning of heating and hot water systems. The person carrying out the work must provide the local authority with a notice confirming that all fixed services have been properly commissioned in accordance with government-approved procedures.

5.17.2 Buildings other than dwellings

New buildings and works to existing buildings will require commissioning of all controlled services (heating, hot water, electrical and mechanical) in accordance with CIBSE Code M[31] by a suitably qualified person, for example a member of the Commissioning Specialists Association or the Commissioning Group of the HVCA.

All ductwork must be tested for air leakage (and, where necessary, remedial work undertaken) in accordance with HVCA DW 143[10] by a suitably qualified person, for example a member of the HVCA Specialist Ductwork Group or the Association of Ductwork Contractors and Allied Services.

An approved competent person must certify commissioning of controlled services. The person carrying out the work must provide the local authority with a notice confirming that all fixed services have been properly commissioned in accordance with a procedure approved by the government.

The requirement for non-dwellings is more onerous than for dwellings as it includes all services and not just ventilation, heating and hot water.

5.18 How to compile an instruction/completion pack

5.18.1 New dwellings

Information must be provided to each dwelling owner, as required by AD L1A Section 6. However, the building's occupier is to be provided with 'sufficient information, including operating and maintenance instructions, enabling the building and the building services to be operated and maintained in such a manner as to consume no more fuel and power than is reasonable in the circumstances'. It would therefore be appropriate that both owner and occupier (if they are not the same person or organisation) are provided with suitable operating instructions.

The actual information to be supplied will depend on the complexity of the dwelling, but the following list should cover most requirements:

- heating system;
- adjustment of boiler temperature (or other heat source);
- setting operating times;
- adjustment of room temperatures (temperature-regulating valves and room thermostat):
  - boiler service interval; and
  - boiler manufacturer's user instructions;
- hot water:
  - adjustment of water temperature;
  - setting operating times; and
  - avoidance of waste;
- ventilation:
  - use of any mechanical and passive ventilation systems;
  - service intervals for mechanical ventilation; and

- – cleaning or replacement of filters;
- lighting:
  - – use of energy-efficient lighting; and
  - – life of lamps and replacement procedure;
- solar gain:
  - – use and maintenance of any solar protection measures provided;
- EPC.
  - – the data used to calculate the TER and the DER;
  - – 'on-construction' EPC; and
  - – the recommendations report that accompanies the EPC.

5.18.2 Works to existing dwellings

Similar requirements apply as for new dwellings in relation to the scope of work to be undertaken, but the information to be provided applies only to the work that has actually been carried out. A SAP assessment is not required by Part L1B except for a material change of use, but may be needed in future as part of sale documentation.

5.18.3 Non-dwellings

An operating and maintenance manual (logbook) is required. The CIBSE publication TM 31[29] provides guidance and standard templates for the content. For work in existing buildings, the information to be provided applies only to the work that has actually been carried out.

For new buildings, the occupier should also be provided with the recommendations report that accompanies the EPC, which sets out how the energy performance of the building might be improved.

Designers should ensure that provision of the operating and maintenance manual is included in the contract specification or the M&E design brief.

5.19 How to assess 'simple payback' over time

When extending a building, or renewing or refurbishing a thermal element (wall, roof or floor), there may be situations where full compliance with an upgrade of U-value is not economic.

If the **simple payback** period is more than 15 years, the upgrade is not required. If the remaining life of the building is less than 15 years, payback is to be calculated only for the remaining life of the building.

> To calculate the payback period:
>
> The payback period in years =
> cost of additional insulation/estimated annual energy saving

Table A1 of Part L1B gives advice on what is likely to be economical where there is little or no existing thermal insulation material provided to the existing thermal element.

Where some thermal insulation is already provided or the upgrade will be unusually expensive, the payback period can be calculated to check if the upgrade is required.

AD L1B 5.7–5.10 and AD L2B 3.1, 'simple payback', state that prices should be current at the date that the proposals are made known to the BCB [current energy prices can be obtained from the Business, Enterprise and Regulatory Reform (BERR) website].[32] The appraisal should be confirmed in a report signed by a suitably qualified person (e.g. a chartered quantity surveyor). The cost including labour and materials can be calculated from contract rates or published price guides.

The estimated annual saving should be obtained by use of SAP for dwellings, or an SBEM or an approved modelling tool for non-dwellings. This may be an additional project cost greater than any potential saving by not insulating.

> The requirement to upgrade applies to the **renovation** of thermal elements. The requirement does not apply to redecoration.

5.20 Low- and zero-carbon energy sources

LZC energy supply systems provide a flexible option for meeting the DER for dwellings/BER for non-dwellings and an opportunity to reduce carbon emissions from existing buildings.

The requirements for LZC energy systems are set out in the *Domestic Building Services Compliance Guide*[4] for dwellings and in the *Non-domestic Building Services Compliance Guide*[21] for non-dwellings. The key requirements are summarised in Table 9.

Table 9
Requirements for LZC energy systems

Dwellings	Non-dwellings
Biomass	*Biomass boilers*
Information within the *Domestic Building Services Compliance Guide*[4] applies to solid fuel heating systems including those that use wood logs, wood pellets or wood chips	The efficiency of biomass boilers at their nominal load should be at least:
	• 65% for independent gravity-fed boilers below 20.5kW
New or replacement systems must meet the minimum standards set out in Table 18 for heating efficiency	• 75% for independent automatic pellet/woodchip boilers
Central heating systems should also have a ratio of room heat to water heat appropriate to the room and property and meet the standards of:	Controls should be as Table 5 of the *Non-domestic Building Services Compliance Guide*[21] where technically feasible
• Table 20 for circulation, fuel and hot water storage, system preparation, water treatment and commissioning	
• Table 21 for controls	
• Table 22 for pipework insulation	
Solar hot water systems	
Information within the *Domestic Building Services Compliance Guide*[4] applies to systems with a collector area of less than 20m² and with storage of less than 440l	
New or replacement systems must meet the minimum standards set out in:	
• Table 37 for certification, testing, transfer fluid, pump power, heat exchanger sizing, controls, storage and system preparation	
• Table 38 for labelling and commissioning	
• Table 39 for insulation of primary pipe work	
Heat pumps	*Heat pumps*
Table 33 of the *Domestic Building Services Compliance Guide*[4] describes the ground-, water- and air-sourced systems covered by the guidance. Systems must:	Table 10 of the *Non-domestic Building Services Compliance Guide*[21] describes the ground-, water- and air-sourced systems covered by the guidance. Systems in new and existing buildings must:
• have a coefficient of performance (CoP) of not less than 2.2 when used for space heating, and no less than 2.0 when producing domestic hot water	• meet the minimum standards set out in Table 11 for CoP
• have a specific fan power no worse than that set out in BS EN 15450 Table C1 for new dwellings and Table C2 for existing dwellings	• meet the requirements for controls set out in Table 12 for new buildings and Table 13 for existing buildings
• meet the minimum standards set out in Table 34 for warm water and hot water heat pumps and Table 35 for warm air heat pumps	

Table 9
Continued

Dwellings	Non-dwellings
Community heating	*Combined heat and power and community heating*
Information within the *Domestic Building Services Compliance Guide*[4] applies to wet heating systems serving 15 or more dwellings and covers systems that connect to a new or an existing community heating scheme	Information within the *Non-domestic Building Services Compliance Guide*[21] applies to CHP systems with an electrical output of less than 500kWe serving commercial applications that may or may not supply community heating
New community heating schemes must meet the minimum standards set out in:	CHP in new and existing buildings should have:
• Table 24 for energy efficiency	• a minimum CHP quality index of 105 and a power efficiency greater than 20% (both under annual operation)
• Table 25 for heat sources	• controls such that the CHP unit operates as lead heat generator
• Table 26 for controls	• metering to measure hours run, electricity generated and input fuel
• Table 27 for hot water production, storage and treatment, metering and commissioning	Standby boilers, where installed, must meet the requirements set out in the *Non-domestic Building Services Compliance Guide*[21]
• Table 28 for pipework insulation	
Existing community heating schemes must meet the minimum standards set out in:	
• Table 26 for controls	
• Table 28 for pipework insulation	
Carbon emission factors should be based on the particular details of the scheme	
Replacement boilers must meet the standards for efficiency set out in the *Non-domestic Building Services Compliance Guide*[21]	

Micro-CHP

Information within the *Domestic Building Services Compliance Guide*[4] applies to systems with an electrical output of less than 5kWe

The heating plant emission ratio (HPER) of a micro-CHP system should be no greater than 0.23kg CO_2/kW·h when calculated using the annual performance method for systems that have been tested to PAS 67[33] using a plant size ratio of 1.5

Table 9
Continued

Dwellings	Non-dwellings
Photovoltaics	*Photovoltaics*
Information within the *Domestic Building Services Compliance Guide*[4] applies to photovoltaic systems with an electrical output of less than 5kWe New or replacement systems must meet the minimum standards set out in: • Table 41 for photovoltaic cell efficiency • Table 42 for ventilation of photovoltaic modules and commissioning	Information within the *Non-domestic Building Services Compliance Guide*[21] applies to photovoltaic systems with an electrical output of greater than 5kWe New or replacement systems should have a conversion efficiency which is no worse than those set out in Table 45 for the various module types
Wind power	*Wind power*
Information within the *Domestic Building Services Compliance Guide*[4] applies to systems in new or existing dwellings that: • do not require three-phase grid connection • have a reference power of less than 50kW at 11m/s wind speed The energy performance for new or replacement systems must be no worse than 175kWh/m2 p.a. for an annual mean wind speed of 5m/s	Information within the *Non-domestic Building Services Compliance Guide*[21] applies to systems in new or existing **dwellings** that: • require three-phase grid connection • have a reference power of less than 50kW at 11m/s wind speed The energy performance for new or replacement systems must be no worse than 175kWh/m2 p.a. for an annual mean wind speed of 5m/s

Notes

1. *The Government's Standard Assessment Procedure for the Energy Rating of Dwellings* (SAP), see http://www.bre.co.uk/sap2009.

2. *National Calculation Methodology (NCM) Modelling Guide (for buildings other than dwellings in England and Wales).* CLG (2010).

3. CIBSE TM 23 *Testing Buildings for Air Leakage.* CIBSE (2000).

4. *Domestic Building Services Compliance Guide.* CLG (2010).

5. The Energy Information (Household Air Conditioners) (No. 2) Regulations. SI 2005/1726.

6. BS 8206-2 *Code of Practice for Daylighting.*

7. BRE Information Paper IP 1/06 *Assessing the Effects of Thermal Bridging at Junctions and around Openings.* BRE (2006).

8. BRE Report BR 262 *Thermal Insulation: Avoiding Risks.* BRE (2001).

9. *Notice of Approval of the Methodology of Calculation of the Energy Performance of Buildings in England and Wales.* CLG (2008).

10. HVCA DW 143 *A Practical Guide to Leakage Testing.* HVCA (2000).

11. *Metering Energy Use in New Non-domestic Buildings.* GIL 65, Carbon Trust (2004).

12. BR 443 *Conventions for U-value Calculations.* BRE (2006).

13. Lstiburek, J. and J. Carmody. *Moisture Control Handbook: Principles and Practices for Residential and Small Commercial Buildings.* London: International Thomson, 1993, xiv, p.214.

14. BS 5250:2002 *Code of Practice for Control of Condensation in Buildings*

15. CIBSE TM 36 *Climate Change and the Indoor Environment – Impacts and Adaptation.* CIBSE (2005).

16. *Solar Shading of Buildings BR 364.* CRC Ltd (1999).

17. *Energy Efficiency Best Practice in Housing: Reducing Overheating – a Designer's Guide.* The Energy Saving Trust (2005).

18. *Air-tightness in Commercial and Public Buildings.* BRE (2002).

19. *Guide to Part F of the Building Regulations, Ventilation.* NBS 2010.

20. *Measuring Air Permeability of Building Envelopes.* ATTMA 2006 (due to be revised 2010).

21. *Non-domestic Building Services Compliance Guide.* CLG (2010).

22. BS 5422:2001 BS 5422:2001 *Method for Specifying Thermal Insulating Materials for Pipes, Tanks, Vessels, Ductwork and Equipment Operating within the Temperature Range of –40°C to +700°C.* (2001).

23. BS EN 253:2003 *District Heating Pipes. Pre-insulated bonded pipe systems for directly buried hot water networks. Pipe assembly of steel service pipe, polyurethane thermal insulation and outer casing of polyethylene.* (2003)

24. CE124/GPG 268 *Energy Efficient Ventilation in Housing. A Guide for Specifiers.* Energy Saving Trust (2006*).*

25. *Domestic Ventilation Compliance Guide.* CLG (2010).

26. HVCA DW 144 *Specifications for Sheet Metal Ductwork.* HVCA (1998)

27. Health Technical Memorandum *HTM 03-01: Specialised Ventilation for Healthcare Premises – Part A: Design and Validation.* DHEFD (2007).

28. Building Bulletin 101 *BB101 Ventilation of School Buildings.* DCSF (2006).

29. CIBSE TM 31 *Building Logbook Toolkit.* CIBSE (2006).

30. BR 497 *Conventions for Calculating Linear Thermal Transmittance and Temperature Factors.* BRE (2007).

31. CIBSE Code M *Commissioning Management.* CIBSE (2003).

32. See http://www.berr.gov.uk/energy/statistics/publications/prices/index.html.

33. PAS 67. *Laboratory Test to Determine Heat and Heat-led Micro-cogeneration Packages Primarily Intended for Heated Dwellings.*

Documents referenced in Part L and what they cover

Document	Synopsis	Reference
BRE Digest DG 498 *Selecting Lighting Controls* (2006)	This digest explains the common types of control, when to use them and how to calculate energy savings	L2A and L2B
BRE Information Paper IP 1/06 *Assessing the Effects of Thermal Bridging at Junctions and around Openings* (2006)	Guidance on thermal bridging and air leakage	L1A and L2A
BRE Report BR 262 *Thermal Insulation: Avoiding Risks* (2001)	Provides detailed guidance by building element on avoiding the risks associated with higher levels of insulation. It includes suggested details for a number of locations	All Parts
BRE Report BR 443 *Conventions for U-value Calculations* (2006)	Guidance on U-value calculations	All Parts
BS 5250:2002 *Code of Practice for Control of Condensation in Buildings*	Guidance on the principles and practice of locating insulation and arranging ventilation to reduce the risk of condensation	L1B
BS 6229:2003 *Flat Roofs with Continuously Supported Coverings. Code of Practice*	General code of practice, but makes reference to thermal design and avoidance of condensation	L1B
BS 8206-2:1992 *Code of Practice for Daylighting*	Guidance on providing adequate daylight while reducing gains by reducing window sizes	L1A and L2A
BS EN ISO 13788:2002 *Hydrothermal Performance of Building Components and Building Elements*	Provides calculation methods to identify risks of condensation, both interstitial and surface	L1B
BSRIA BG 8/2009 *Model Commissioning Plan*	Guidance on documenting commissioning	L1A

Document	Synopsis	Reference
Building Regulations and Historic Buildings, English Heritage 2002 (rev. 2004)	Guidance on the application of Part L to buildings that are listed or have architectural or historic interest	L1B and L2B
Commissioning Code M: Commissioning Management, CIBSE (2003)	Commissioning procedure for non-domestic **building works**	L2A and L2B
Domestic Building Services Compliance Guide, CLG (2010)	Describes requirements for compliance with L1A and L1B for heating and hot water services, associated controls, pipework, lighting and LZC energy sources	L1A and L1B
HVCA DW 143 *A Practical Guide to Ductwork Leakage Testing*, HVCA (2000)	Procedure required with fan flow rates greater than $1m^3/s$	L2A and L2B
HVCA DW 144 *Specifications for Sheet Metal Ductwork – Low, Medium and High Pressure/Velocity Air Systems* (Appendix M revision 2002), HVCA (1998)	Contains recognised UK standard specifications for ductwork manufacture and installation	L2A
HVCA DW 144 *Specifications for Sheet Metal Ductwork* (1998)	Provides a means to demonstrating compliance with air leakage requirements	L2A and L2B
Measuring Air Permeability of Building Envelopes, ATTMA (2006)	Standards and methods for testing air permeability of buildings	L1A and L2A
NCM Modelling Guide (for buildings other than dwellings in England and Wales), CLG (2008)	Provides guidance on the use of SBEM and other approved software	L2A and L2B
Non-domestic Building Services Compliance Guide, CLG (2010)	Describes requirements for compliance with L2A and L2B for heating, hot water, cooling and ventilation services, associated controls, pipework, lighting and LZC energy sources. It contains a compliance checklist and a schedule of data required for Input into the NCM tool	L2A and L2B
SBEM User Manual and Calculation Tool, BRE (2006) http://www.ncm.bre.co.uk	Calculation tool to demonstrate the energy requirements of a building using the SBEM	L1A and L2A

Document	Synopsis	Reference
The Government's Standard Assessment Procedure for Energy Rating of Dwellings, BRE/DECC (http://www.bre.co.uk/ sap2009)	Guidance on (SAP) calculation of CO_2 emissions in domestic buildings	L1A
Thermal Insulation of H & V Ductwork, TIMSA (1998)	Sets the standards for insulating pipes, ducts and vessels	L2A and L2B
TM 36 *Climate Change and the Internal Environment – Impacts and Adaptation*, CIBSE (2005)	Guidance on the need to improve the passive performance of buildings to reduce the need for cooling in future	L1A and L2A
TM 31 *Building Logbook Toolkit*, CIBSE (2006)	Guide to a compliant building logbook, showing data required	L2A and L2B
TM 37 *Design for Improved Solar Shading Control*, CIBSE (2006)	Guidance on the design of façades to incorporate appropriate levels of solar shading, also information on some design options	L2A
TM 39 *Building Energy Metering (a Guide to Energy Sub-metering in Non-domestic Buildings)*, CIBSE (2009)	An updated version of General Information Leaflet 65	L2A and L2B
TM 46 *Energy Benchmarks*, CIBSE (2008)	Contains energy benchmarks for various building types and provides details of separable energy uses	L2A and L2B

Glossary

Accredited construction details (ACDs)	An approach to encourage the take-up of specific proprietary details, as developed by industry, for both the dwellings and the non-domestic sectors. ACDs cover: • air-barrier continuity; • thermal insulation; • vapour control See 5.16 of this guide
Accredited SAP assessor	A person who operates under an accreditation scheme approved by the government
Approved calculation tool	A government-approved methodology for rating the energy efficiency of new buildings. For dwellings, the approved calculation tool is SAP. In other buildings, this means SBEM or another calculation tool that is accredited as complying with the NCM
Approved competent person	Schemes introduced by the government to allow individuals and enterprises to self-certify that their work complies with the building regulations as an alternative to submitting a building notice or using an approved inspector. A list of bodies authorised to operate competent person schemes is available from CLG's website[1]
ATTMA	Air Tightness Testing and Measurement Association (a special interest group within the British Institute of Non-Destructive Testing)
Building emission rate (BER)	The amount of CO_2 in kilograms emitted per square metre of floor area per year as the result of the provision of heating, cooling, hot water, ventilation and internal fixed lighting. This may be in the form of a prediction at design stage or a prediction based on the as-built dwelling, taking into account the results of air permeability tests. It is calculated using the SAP energy calculation tool. Refer to Appendix 5.3

Building work	In the context of the Building Regulations, building work means: (a) the erection or extension of a building; (b) the provision or extension of a **controlled service** or **controlled fitting** in or in connection with a building; (c) the material alteration of a building, or a controlled service or fitting, as mentioned in b; (d) work required by Regulation 6 (requirements relating to material change of use); (e) the insertion of insulating material into the cavity wall of a building; and (f) work involving the underpinning of a building *See also* material alteration
Change in energy status	Any change that results in a building becoming a building to which the energy efficiency requirements of the Building Regulations apply, where previously it was not
Commissioning specialist	Member of the Commissioning Specialists Association or the Commissioning Group of the HVCA
Consequential improvement works	Work that is triggered as a requirement to the existing building as a consequence of: (a) extending an existing building over 1000m²; (b) the initial provision of fixed building services; or (c) increasing the installed capacity of an existing building service The works that trigger the need for consequential works are called the **principal works**. The cost of consequential works should meet the requirements of simple payback calculations and should not be less than 10% of the cost of the principal works (unless the existing building already meets the required thermal performance)
Conservatory	An extension that is thermally separated from the attached building by walls, windows and doors with U-value and draught-stripping provisions no worse than provided elsewhere in the building, and, if a heating system is provided, that system has independent temperature and on/off controls, and where the area of transparent or translucent material in its external envelope parts is more than 150% of its floor area
Controlled fittings	Controlled fittings are windows (including the glazed elements of a curtain wall), roof lights and doors (including high-usage doors, large access doors for vehicles and roof ventilators) but not display windows
Controlled services	Heating and hot water systems, pipes and ducts, mechanical ventilation or cooling, fixed internal lighting including display lighting and occupier-controlled external lighting

Dwelling	A self-contained unit designed to accommodate a single household. Rooms for residential purposes are not dwellings, so Part L2A is applicable to their construction
Dwelling emission rate (DER)	The amount of CO_2 in kilograms emitted per square metre of floor area per year as the result of the provision of heating, hot water, ventilation and internal (and occupier-controlled external) fixed lighting. It can be calculated on a per **dwelling** basis or averaged over all the dwellings in a block. DER is both a prediction at design stage and a subsequent prediction based on the as-built dwelling, taking into account the results of air permeability tests. It is calculated using the SAP energy calculation tool. Refer to Appendices 5.2 and 5.4
Extension to a dwelling	An addition to a dwelling. Exemptions apply where the extension is a carport that is open on at least two sides. Where the extension is a conservatory or a porch of less than 30m², Part L applies but the works are not notifiable
Fit-out works	The fitting-out of the shell of a building for occupation as an independently procured piece of work. The first fit-out of a building should be treated as part of the new works, even if there is a delay between completing the shell and the commencement of the fit-out works, including where the shell is sold or let before the fit-out work is carried out
Historic buildings	Buildings, including listed buildings, that are referred to in the local authority's development plan as being of local architectural or historic interest, or those buildings in national parks, areas of outstanding natural beauty and world heritage sites and to which *specific guidance applies*. When dealing with a historic building, refer to the English Heritage Guidance Note *Building Regulations and Historic Buildings* (English Heritage 2002)[2]
Low- and zero-carbon (LZC) energy supply systems	Renewable and other low-carbon energy sources, such as absorption cooling, ground cooling, biomass, CHP, ground source heat pumps, wind energy, and photovoltaic and solar hot water
Material alteration	An alteration that results in reduced compliance with certain parts of the Building Regulations. This could arise at any stage in the works, including (presumably) construction. An alteration is material for the purposes of these Regulations if the work, or any part of it, would at any stage result in: a) a building, controlled service or fitting not complying with a relevant requirement where previously it did; or b) a building, controlled service or fitting that, before the work commenced, did not comply with a relevant requirement being more unsatisfactory in relation to such a requirement

Material alteration (continued)

In connection with the above relevant requirement are any of the following applicable requirements of Schedule 1, namely:

- Part A (structure);
- paragraph B1 (means of warning and escape);
- paragraph B3 (internal fire spread – structure);
- paragraph B4 (external fire spread); and
- paragraph B5 (access and facilities for the fire service); and
- Part M (access and facilities for disabled people)

Material change of use

For the purposes of the Regulations, a change in the purposes for which, or the circumstances in which, a building is used, so that after that change:

(a) the building is used as a dwelling, where previously it was not (use Part L1B);

(b) the building contains a flat, where previously it did not (use Part L1B);

(c) the building is used as a hotel or boarding house, when previously it was not (use Part L2B);

(d) the building is used as an institution, where previously it was not (use Part L2B);

(e) the building is used as a public building, where previously it was not (use Part L2B);

(f) the building is not a building described in Classes I to VI in Schedule 2, where previously it was (Part L no longer applies);

(g) the building, which contains at least one dwelling, contains a greater or lesser number of dwellings than it did previously (use Part L1B);

(h) the building contains a room for residential purposes, where previously it did not (use Part L1B if the room is a dwelling, for example a caretaker's flat; use Part L2B if the residential use is not a dwelling, such as a hostel);

(i) the building, which contains at least one room for residential purposes, contains a greater or lesser number of rooms than it did previously (use Part L1B if the room is a dwelling, e.g. a caretaker's flat; use Part L2B if the residential use is not a dwelling, such as a hostel);

(j) the building is used as a shop, where previously it was not (use Part L2B)

Principal works

Principal works means the work necessary to achieve the client's purposes in extending the building and/or increasing the installed capacity of any fixed building services. The value of the principal works is the basis for determining a reasonable provision of consequential improvements

Qualified inspector	The National Association of Professional Inspectors and Testers provides an independent professional trade body for electrical inspectors, electrical contractors, electricians and allied trades throughout the UK. The National Inspection Council for Electrical Installation Contracting is the industry's independent, non-profit-making, voluntary regulatory body
Reasonable provision	Shorthand for reasonable means to provide compliant solutions under the Building Regulations, and for which the ADs were originally conceived. These provisions are not mandatory if alternative solutions can be demonstrated to meet the requirements of the Building Regulations. Bear in mind that the CO_2 emission target to be achieved is mandatory
Renovation	In relation to a **thermal element**, the process of stripping down the element to expose the basic structural components (brick/blockwork/ timber/metal frame/ joists/rafters, etc.) and then rebuilding to achieve all the necessary performance requirements. Renovation applies only where the area to be refurbished is greater than one of the following limits (smaller proportions being regarded as repairs): 50% of the surface of the individual element; 25% of the total building envelope [to be consistent with the Energy Performance of Buildings Directive (EPBD) requirement]
Second-tier documents	Documents such as the *Domestic Building Services Compliance Guide*[3] that contain the detailed requirements referred to in the ADs (the first-tier documents)
Simple payback	The amount of time it will take to recover the initial investment through energy savings. It is calculated by dividing the marginal additional cost of implementing an energy efficiency measure by the value of energy savings achieved by that measure. This is based on current prices excluding VAT [current energy prices can be obtained from the BERR (Department for Business Enterprise and Regulatory Reform) website][4] calculated by a suitably qualified person. There is an example of how to work out simple payback in Appendix 5.19 of this guide
Suitably qualified person	Suitably qualified persons can certify that work complies with building regulations. For pressure testing, one example of a suitably qualified person would be an ATTMA member. For commissioning, an example would be a member of the Commissioning Specialists Association or the Commissioning Group of the HVCA in respect of HVAC systems, or a member of the Lighting Industry Commissioning Scheme in respect of fixed internal or external lighting. For demonstration of simple payback or cost of consequential improvements, a suitably qualifed person is the equivalent of a chartered quantity surveyor. Other examples are individuals and enterprises that have registered with the Competent Person Schemes introduced by the government to allow them to self-certify that their work complies with the Building Regulations. These are identified on the CLG website.

Target emission rate (TER)	The target amount of CO_2 in kilograms emitted per square metre of floor area per year as the result of the provision of heating, hot water, cooling, ventilation and internal fixed lighting based on the CO_2 emissions from a notional building of the same size and shape as proposed with an improvement factor applied. In non-dwellings, the TER can also be adjusted to take account of LZC energy sources. Refer to Appendix 5.1 for details
Thermal element	A wall (including the opaque elements of a curtain wall), floor, ceiling or roof that separates internal conditioned space from the external environment
Third-tier documents	Documents such as industry guidance, good practice guides, codes of practice and standards
Useful floor area	The gross floor area as measured in accordance with the guidance issued by the RICS (Royal Institution of Chartered Surveyors) – the total area of all enclosed spaces measured to the internal face of the external walls. It is described in the ADs as the total area of all enclosed spaces measured to the internal face of the external walls. The area of sloping surfaces such as staircases, galleries, raked auditoria and tiered terraces should be taken as their area on plan. It should include areas occupied by partitions, column chimney breasts and internal structural or party walls. It excludes areas not enclosed such as open floors, covered ways and balconies (L2B, paragraph 112)

Notes

1. See http://www.communities.gov.uk/planningandbuilding/buildingregulations/competentpersons-schemes/
2. *Building Regulations and Historic Buildings*. English Heritage (2002, revised 2004).
3. *Domestic Building Services Compliance Guide*. CLG (2010).
4. See http://www.berr.gov.uk/energy/statistics/publications/prices/index.html.

Index

The following abbreviations have been used:
    BER, building emission rate
    DER, dwelling emission rate
    TER, target emission rate

NOT TO BE
TAKEN AWAY

181592